Chucks!

Chucks!

The Phenomenon of Converse:
Chuck Taylor All Stars

Hal Peterson

Skyhorse Publishing

Skyhorse Publishing books may be purchased in bulk at special discounts for sales promotion, corporate gifts, fund-raising, or educational purposes. Special editions can also be created to specifications. For details, contact the Special Sales Department, Skyhorse Publishing, 307 West 36th Street, 11th Floor, New York, NY 10018 or info@skyhorsepublishing.com.

Skyhorse® and Skyhorse Publishing® are registered trademarks of Skyhorse Publishing, Inc.®, a Delaware corporation.

Visit our website at www.skyhorsepublishing.com.

10 9 8 7 6 5 4 3 2 1

Library of Congress Cataloging-in-Publication Data is available on file.

Cover design by DILONÉ

Print ISBN: 978-1-5107-0221-9
Ebook ISBN: 978-1-5107-0258-5

Printed in China

Contents

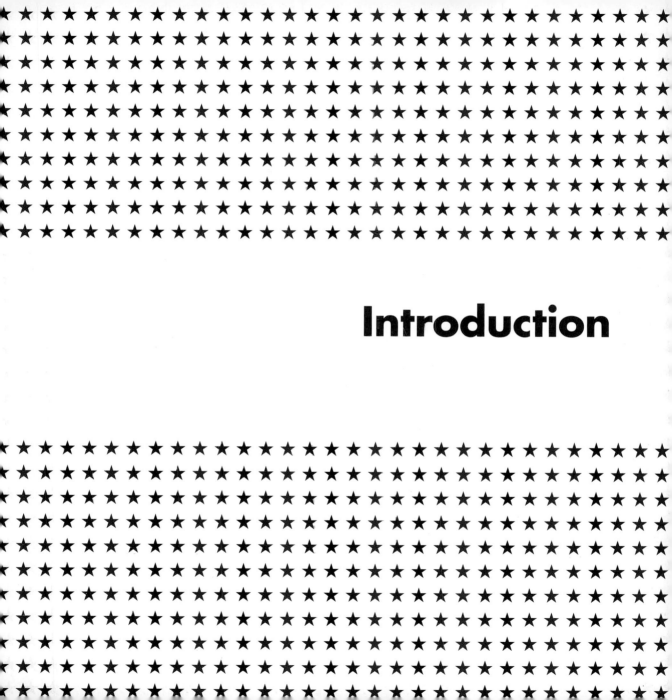

Introduction

WHAT ARE CHUCKS? If you have never owned a pair, you may be asking this question. "Chucks" is the popular slang term for the Converse Chuck Taylor All Star basketball shoe, the world's most enduring and popular athletic footwear. People who are dedicated to wearing chucks never just call them sneakers; chucks have always been a step apart from common or generic athletic shoes.

The anatomy of a pair of high-top chucks.

The basic design of a typical pair of high-top chucks is simple yet brilliant. You start with two rubber outer soles with a unique pattern of lines and diamonds underneath half-moon toe caps, attach two-layer canvas uppers and a tongue to each outer sole, add a spongy rubber and fabric insole, and then connect them all together with a white outer wrap accented with colored piping and a toe guard with more embedded diamonds and lines. Each shoe has seven, eight, or nine pairs of metal eyelets that are used to hold the flat, stretchable shoelaces, plus two on the inside for "ventilation." The shoes are completed with double rows of stitching along the edges, below the eyelets, and up the back, and ankle support is provided by a third piece of canvas. A circular patch made of thin rubber containing a bright blue star, the words "Converse All Star," and the signature of Chuck Taylor is glued to the inside ankle point of each shoe. A heel patch on the back of each shoe has a star set between the words "All" and "Star." Their intricate geometric patterns and shapes, durability and functionality, and sleek modern look make your pair of chucks a perfect example of the Art Deco style that was fashionable in America and Europe at the time chucks were first designed and manufactured.

Chucks are an American classic; they are recognized around the world. A pair of chucks is housed in the Smithsonian, but the shoes are also still worn by millions of people who consider them to be contemporary fashion. First sold in 1917, the shoes evolved to their present look over the next several decades. During this time, three main models—an all-black canvas high-top, a 1936 Olympics–inspired white high-top with red and blue trim, and an all-black leather high-top—were manufactured. After World War II, the black canvas shoes were changed from their monochrome design to the present black-and-white look, which features white laces, toe caps, and outer wraps in contrast to the black canvas uppers. By 1948, All Stars had the same appearance as the core high-top models produced today. In 1957, the low-cut All Star oxford model was introduced.

1936 Converse ad for Chuck Taylor All Stars.

3

Charles "Chuck" Taylor around the time of his induction into the Basketball Hall of Fame.

In their first five decades, Converse All Stars became established as the premier model of basketball shoe, extensively promoted by a man named Charles Chuck Taylor. Taylor was a skilled basketball player, clinician, and coach who made some significant design changes to the shoes after he came to work for Converse in 1921. Taylor was rewarded for his efforts in the 1930s when his name was added to the product and his signature was placed on its ankle patch. The 1940s, '50s, and '60s were the glory years for the Converse Chuck Taylor All Star. Almost all high school, college, and professional teams wore Converse Olympic white, black leather, or black canvas basketball shoes.

In 1969, Taylor was inducted into the Basketball Hall of Fame, and later that year he passed away from a heart attack. Maybe this was a premonition of the dramatic changes that were coming to the athletic shoe industry. In the 1970s, competition from new companies such as Nike, Reebok, and adidas made inroads into the dominance of the Converse Company. Without the tireless salesmanship of Chuck Taylor, the company lost market share to its competitors and their new technological high-performance innovations. Basketball teams stopped wearing Converse shoes in favor of other brands. As a result, the role of the Chuck Taylor All Star began to evolve. In the last three decades of the twentieth century, and into the twenty-first century, chucks have been known more as a leisure and lifestyle shoe, now available in hundreds of different colors and patterns and in high-top, low-cut, slip-on, and knee-high styles.

Chucks are a true unisex shoe; they have always been a basketball shoe for women as well as men. These days, chucks are equally popular among men and women as a fashion statement. Liana Aghajanian, a young newspaper reporter, once described chucks to me as "the great unifier." From film celebrities to the kid next door, business professionals to musicians in rock bands, guys in college to teenage girls who cruise the mall looking for the latest models, chucks are proudly worn by people from many different age groups and demographic categories. What they have in common is their love and affection for the comfort and look of these shoes, along with their desire to wear them as much as possible.

Christmas card snapshot for the Tom Andrews family.

After starting **The ChucksConnection** (www.chucksconnection.com), a website for enthusiasts of the Chuck Taylor shoe to exchange photographs and information, I discovered that there was a lot more to the story of the Converse Chuck Taylor All Star than people lacing up different models. Chucks are a phenomenon in our society and have had a cultural impact that has been noted in our visual and print media. They have influenced fashion, music, and sports in America and throughout the world. As our information about chucks has expanded,

Corporate IT team for SWCA wearing their chucks.

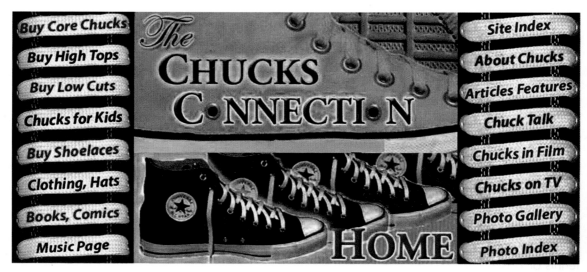

The ChucksConnection home page

thanks to the contributions of many devoted chucks fans throughout the world, these subjects have become well documented on **The ChucksConnection** website. Throughout this book, conclusions from this research will be presented.

An excellent illustration of the impact of chucks on our society was seen in January 2001, when the management of Converse declared bankruptcy and it looked as though the end was near for the Chuck Taylor shoe. Newspapers and magazines were flooded with articles lamenting the loss of this great cultural icon, and there was a run on the remaining stock in stores. Although the bankruptcy did result in the loss of "Made in USA" chucks, the Converse and Chuck Taylor brand names were too well established for someone else not to seize the

★

opportunity and reorganize the company. Under new management, emphasis was placed on replenishing the supply of Converse's premier product, the Chuck Taylor All Star, in its core models and seasonal variations. Since then, chucks have become more popular than ever and now have a significant impact on the bottom line of the company's current owners—Nike, Inc.

Where did the word "chucks" come from? "Chucks" has been a slang word in the English vernacular for hundreds of years and has had many different meanings. In the past three decades, a new meaning for "chucks" has emerged: a noun denoting a pair of Chuck Taylor shoes. This term has been used in published articles, has become a common word in everyday conversation, and has been listed in reference works such as Jonathan Green's *The Dictionary of Contemporary Slang*. At **The ChucksConnection**, we believe that the term first came into general usage in the early 1970s, when athletic shoes became popular daily footwear in all segments of society, not just for athletes or kids. There were no longer just all-purpose tennis or basketball shoes. Now there were special athletic shoes designed and marketed for different activities like running and training, along with shoes specifically designed for sports like football, soccer, baseball, and basketball.

With the arrival of many competing models from Nike, Reebok, and adidas, Converse had to react and started coming up with new shoe designs like the Dr. J leather basketball shoe. Up until then, you could use "Converse" or "Cons" to describe Chuck Taylor shoes, and everyone would know what you were talking about. With many models to choose from, and with the public becoming so "sneaker-aware," different names began to emerge to describe popular models. The companies all used endorsements to market the newer shoes, and these names were associated with that product, often in a shortened or abbreviated form. In those days, people who continued to wear original Chuck Taylor shoes didn't have a highly paid celebrity endorser, but being a loyal lot, they just started using the term "chucks" to describe their

Sage Fulton stocking boxes of Chuck Taylor shoes.

favorite shoes, after the shoes' now-deceased designer.

Interestingly, Converse never has used the word "chucks" as a product name for Chuck Taylor shoes. They have always been sold as Converse All Star basketball or athletic shoes. Sometimes you see the words "Chuck Taylor" or "CT" on the boxes, but most models just say "Converse All Star." In just the last couple of years, Converse has started to use the word "Chuck" in some of their advertising copy, but not as a product name. The company took out a trademark on the word "Chucks" about twenty years ago, but that was for a line of clothing products that was only offered for a short time. Furthermore, the correct use of a trademark is as an adjective, not a noun. To enforce such a trademark as a noun would require constant advertising and promotion to keep it in the public mind. Just ask the Coca-Cola Company how much they spend a year reinforcing the idea that "Coke" is a noun that refers to their soft drink product.

So the word "chucks" is really the people's word for these canvas shoes. In recent decades, public usage of the word "chucks" as a noun referring to a pair of original Chuck Taylor shoes has continued to increase globally and independently, in conversations, and in the media.

These days, when you talk about your chucks, most people already understand what you are talking about. If they don't, just point to your shoes!

One final note about the spelling of the word "chucks": it doesn't need to be capitalized. A lot of people do when they write the word, maybe out of respect for Chuck Taylor, but "Chuck" is his nickname, not "Chucks." If it's meant to be possessive, as in "Chuck's shoes," where is the apostrophe and the second word? It's not the formal product name, either. The word "chucks" is slang for a pair of shoes. Since that is not a proper name, the word isn't capitalized here or on **The ChucksConnection** website.

Just point to your shoes!

This is the second edition of *Chucks! The Phenomenon of Converse: Chuck Taylor All Stars.* Since the first edition in 2007, there have been many new models of chucks, significant changes in the way chucks are marketed, and a continued presence in the media and the everyday lives of the millions of people worldwide who wear chucks. These trends will be explored in this updated chucks story.

chapter one

Phenomenal Fans

PEOPLE WHO WEAR chucks come from all segments of society. Chucks are regularly worn by people of all ages, by celebrities and regular folk, and by people with all types of occupations and interests. If you look around, you see chucks on the feet of the rich, the middle class, and the poor. Chucks are daily footwear for men, women, boys, and girls. Chuck Taylor shoes have been worn by millions of people from different backgrounds and ethnicities. High school, college, and professional basketball players wore them on the court for over fifty years. Baby boomers wore them as kids and continue to wear them as adults. Chucks have been a favorite shoe of musicians in bands for decades. Chucks are worn by our newer generations to make a fashion statement. Chucks are the shoes of people advocating alternative lifestyles and the shoes of mainstream America.

Chucks are worn by all types of people (above). Some of the millions of chucks (right).

At least 60 percent of all Americans own at least one pair of chucks in their lifetime. There have been more than nine hundred million pairs sold, making chucks the number one athletic shoe in America. They were one of the first mass-produced athletic shoes and have been continuously

manufactured since 1917. Today, thousands of pairs of chucks are sold each week worldwide. Soon they will be like McDonald's, advertising over one billion sold. The amazing thing about chucks is that this simple shoe continues to appeal to each generation, and the fan base of dedicated chucks wearers continues to increase. People who like chucks show an unparalleled loyalty to the product, a fact that is especially remarkable when you list all of the possible footwear choices these days and the lack of mainstream advertising by Converse. It's no accident that one of Converse's advertising slogans for the Chuck Taylor All Star was "Stay True."

★

Insiders and Outsiders

ONE OF THE IRONIES you discover when examining the history of chucks is that they have been the favored athletic shoe for both "insiders" and "outsiders." During their first fifty years, chucks were recognized as the premier basketball shoe, sought after by top players and those who aspired to be the best. Owning a pair of chucks was a special moment in a young athlete's life—you had arrived, and your "limousines for the feet" were worn with pride. There are many stories about young boys scheming to get a pair of real Converse chucks, and of how disappointed they would be if they had to settle for "buddies" or any other second-rate "wannabe"

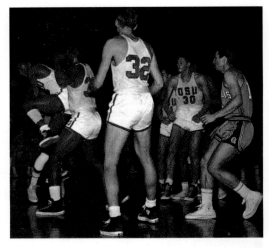

College basketball game from the 1960s.

pair of cheaper basketball shoes. It was a big deal to get together the money for a pair of chucks, when you could buy a competitor's sneaker for half the cost.

Then in the 1970s, when basketball players and teams started gravitating away from wearing chucks, the shoes started being popular with the counterculture, especially among rock musicians and other people who wanted to show that they weren't part of the establishment. Matt Chittum described it best: "They were a symbol of membership in the brotherhood of counterculture, a vulcanized heel with which to mash the penny-loafered toe of convention." Chucks were now available in a rainbow of colors and patterns, allowing for a wide variety of individualized looks. Best of all, chucks were a shoe that would wear well and look cool even when worn to tatters. Because the design of chucks hadn't changed, their price remained stable while the prices of high-performance athletic shoes skyrocketed. This had great appeal to students and others with limited incomes, and now part of the allure of chucks was their low price.

Chucks Make a Fashion Statement

THESE DAYS, WEARING chucks can represent about just anything you want. If you want the classic look (still the bestseller), wear a pair of black high-tops or low-cuts. If you want to adopt the hip-hop look, wear a pair of two- or three-color foldovers. If you want to make a political statement, wear a pair of John Lennon "peace," American flag, or democracy

chucks. If you want to support the military, wear a pair of camouflage chucks. If you want to get people's attention, wear a pair of red, orange, or bright green chucks. If you want to dress conservatively, wear black monochrome chucks. If you like the well-worn grunge look, wear a pair of "distressed" or "rummage" chucks. People who like wearing chucks usually start with one favorite pair in a certain color, but with so many core and seasonal models available to choose from, your typical chucks enthusiast soon acquires several pairs and gets into "wearing the colors."

Collage of different models, including black core, camouflage, peace, flag, comic print, monochrome black, and seasonal colors.

★

In the past fifteen years, chucks have made inroads in the fashion industry. Once dismissed as a low-fashion shoe for kids or out-of-touch adults, the Chuck Taylor All Star is now recognized as a shoe that will lighten up your look, give you some "rock star" credibility, and allow you to mix formal wear with casual wear for an interesting balance of high and low fashion. This new view among fashion insiders and celebrities who follow popular trends is part of the reason that you see so many more young women and teenaged girls wearing chucks now.

For those who wear chucks as their main shoe of choice, any occasion is an appropriate one for wearing chucks and every type of clothing looks good with chucks. You see them worn at

Tom DeLonge from Blink-182 wearing black low-cut chucks (left).
Newspaper supplement ad showing fashion for juniors and young girls (center).
Couple dressed up in chucks (right).

symphony concerts and theatrical productions, by wedding parties and at senior proms, at church services and funerals. You see them worn in the classroom by both teachers and students, out in the country by those hiking nature trails and wading streams, by people playing all kinds of sports or just walking. You see them worn with business suits and tuxedos, with khaki pants and polo shirts, with shorts and sweatshirts, with ragged jeans and torn T-shirts.

Why do Chucks Wearers Remain Loyal?

AT **THE CHUCKSCONNECTION**, we hear from many long-time wearers of chucks. When you ask them why they continue to wear them, you get comments like, "Chuck Taylors are the best shoes in the world," "They are the coolest shoe style ever," "I like the look of high-top chucks," "They're lightweight shoes that breathe well," "I will wear chucks as long as they are made," and "You instantly have something in common with others who wear chucks, and we all notice each other." Stores that sell chucks are aware of this brand loyalty. As Doug Plocki, a shoe store employee commented, "The people who come in to buy them are usually the ones who have a pair already on."

Dedicated fans are aware of the life cycle that each pair of chucks goes through. Going through the various stages of wear is part of the pleasure of wearing chucks. When you first lace up a brand-new pair, the laces, toe guards, toe caps, and outer wrap are a pristine white in color. As a pair begins to age through wear, the laces start to darken from daily exposure to dirt and the color of the canvas uppers. The toe caps and outer wrap begin to lose their bright sheen and pick up dirt stains. The diamond patterns on the outer soles start wearing down

★

to flat squares, and the insoles conform to the shape of your feet. In a few months, when the shoes are fully broken in, the canvas uppers are barely noticeable on your feet, the laces have creased and marked corners where the laces meet the eyelets, and the inner canvas starts to wear in places. On the rubber parts of the shoe, the diamonds and lines on the toe guards start to wear down to a smooth surface, the outer soles show wear places on the lines, and the diamonds are pretty much worn down to solid square blocks. For some people, this is the time to start thinking about getting another pair; for others, this pair of chucks is just starting to

reach the glory days of its grunge look. Depending on how you treat them, and how often you wear them, pairs of chucks can last six months to a year, and even multiple years. When a pair of chucks has reached the end of its daily-wear life, it often has a second life, because most people will keep their used chucks around "in case of emergency" or because a well-worn pair is a souvenir of good times in the past. Old pairs are also great for yard work, painting, river rafting, or other activities where you don't want to mess up a new pair.

The devotion that people have for their chucks is something that is hard to explain. You just don't see it expressed for other footwear or fashionable items. If the word "cult" didn't have so many negative meanings associated with it, you could use the word to describe the feelings that

Green Day drummer Tre Cool (above).
Brand-new pair of black high-tops with box (left).

Well-worn chucks.

dedicated wearers have about chucks. One of the definitions of cult is "something popular or fashionable among a devoted group of enthusiasts." Ironically, one of the interesting things about chucks wearers is that they belong to all kinds of very different political, religious, and social organizations, embrace establishment and alternative lifestyles, can be very hip, fashion-oriented, part of the counterculture, nerd-like, or just regular folks. Perhaps the unifying fascination with chucks that draws all these disparate types together is their unsophisticated simplicity of design and function. Chucks have no pretensions or fancy airs about them. In this era of high technology and constant change, chucks are the shoes that never change.

Why do people like chucks?

WITH SO MANY TYPES of people wearing chucks these days, it's hard to pin down just a few reasons why they like them. You could start the discussion by saying that chucks are great conversation starters, especially among the folks who wear them. "Cool-looking chucks" will always get a response, and some people say that one of the things they like about being in the "chucks club" is the friendships formed with others who wear chucks. Bill Storer, a long-time wearer, describes their allure: "Chucks are maverick sneaks. They separate us from the dull sneaker herd." Brett Staggs describes his feelings about chucks in an interview with Regis Behe of the *Pittsburgh Tribune-Review.* "They emit an aura of sorts. They cause a ripple in the air that everyone feels when you walk by in them. And most of the time, you're not even wearing All Stars—All Stars are wearing you." Staggs, who is the

drummer in the Cool Grand, a local Pittsburgh band, goes on to say, "They're simple, they're smart, they're functional, they're frugal, they're decadent, they're humble, they're selfish, and the size of the shoe is in an easy-to-read place on the bottom. That's why I love All Stars. They are hands down the coolest shoe ever made."

Chucks are also responsible for people wanting to sniff their athletic shoes. One of the most noticeable things about a new pair of Made in USA chucks was their strong smell of vulcanized rubber. Just like new car smell, it would last for a while until your pair started to get worn and broken in. Unfortunately, that rubberized smell is now lost when you buy a new pair made in Asia. The rubber formula has been altered somehow and mixed with what the product label describes as "textile," so there is no more pungent aroma of a newly minted outer sole when you open the box these days.

Three of the seven wonders of the world.

Here are a dozen more reasons why people like chucks

1 **Chucks appeal to our youth culture.** Chucks are always being "discovered" again by the next generation. Regardless of what brand they actually wear, surveys have shown that the large majority of young people think of chucks as cool, inexpensive shoes. By wearing a pair of chucks, young people instantly have something in common

Kicking back in a pair of broken in chucks.

with others who wear them. People who wear chucks notice each other, because the brand of athletic shoes you wear is a big deal in today's youth culture. With so many models and colors to choose from, a young person can show individuality or conformity with a large number of chucks-wearing subgroups, or wear them in a way that makes a lifestyle statement. This youth appeal doesn't end at age twenty-one or even thirty. A very common comment from older people who wear chucks is, "They make me feel young again."

★ ★

2

Chucks are classic style. Classic style is simple, restrained, and refined. All elements are balanced. The Converse Chuck Taylor All Star, especially in its high-top model, is the classic athletic shoe because its blend of boldly colored canvas uppers; rows of stitching; distinctive patches on the inside, heel, or tongue; white flashing on the side; unique footprint; and black, red, or blue piping is perfectly balanced. The chucks look has great visual appeal and is easily recognized by the general public. Chucks complement many types of

Old pairs in a closet.

★

clothing, and because they are a classic, they will never go out of style. There have been modifications over the years since Converse All Stars were first introduced in 1917, but the original design was so good it appears to be timeless.

3 Chucks are comfortable. Fans of chucks seem united on this point: the shoes are very comfortable to wear. Some typical comments: "Once you get used to them, you don't like wearing anything else." "They're real comfortable and lightweight . . . not clunky." "You almost feel like you're barefoot." "Chucks are the only shoe that treat my feet right." Another consensus opinion about chucks is that they get even more comfortable as you continue to wear a pair and they become molded to your feet: "They're not so much a shoe as they are a foot glove." Chucks have been criticized in the past for not having enough arch support. But now the thinking on that point has changed, with new research showing that it is better for your feet to walk in lightweight footwear and mold their own support, which is the experience you get wearing a pair of chucks. Converse did spend a lot of time and money developing their "comfort arch" insole, and apparently what worked fifty years ago is still good today. "They are super comfortable—super individualistic—my second skin and alter ego."

The joy of lacing up new chucks.

4 Chucks are durable. While initially it might seem to be an exaggeration to state that a canvas-and-rubber shoe can last a long time, chucks have always been well made, with a very low failure rate. This is due to eighty years of experience manufacturing them, and also to key modifications in design, production techniques, and materials over the years that improved the quality without changing their basic look. A lot of concern about the quality of chucks was expressed when the manufacturing was taken from the US and moved to Asia. Although there are still some people unhappy about this move and some of the changes in the materials used to make chucks, most people are happy about the quality of the shoes, the new variety of models, and their availability. There are also a few tricks people can use to make their chucks last longer, like alternating pairs and letting them dry out completely before wearing them again. Many long-time wearers of chucks still keep pairs that they have had for many years. "I still wear them," says Sam Cordova of Dallas, Texas. "Some of them are pretty old and they're still in real good condition. That's why I buy them. They last a long time."

5 **Chucks represent freedom from the mundane world.** If there is such a thing as a "philosophy of footwear," you soon discover that wearing a pair of chucks represents freedom: freedom from the world of work (although these days many people are fortunate enough to be able to wear them at work), freedom of expression (with many colors and styles to choose from to express your individuality), freedom from heavy boots and shoes that weigh your feet down, and the freedom associated with summers and vacations. Wearing chucks can make a difference in your life. Many people have commented on what a pleasurable moment it was when they laced up a pair of chucks for the very first time. That special feeling is one of the reasons that people continue to wear chucks throughout their lives.

6 **Chucks are great for special activities.** While most people think of their chucks as a fun casual or athletic shoe, some people like to wear chucks for special

Driving a car wearing chucks.

activities. One devoted wearer of black high-tops states that he prefers to drive his high performance car wearing chucks. "My chucks mold perfectly to the shape of the gas, brake, and
clutch pedals. The rubber sole is just thick and firm enough to prevent puncturing, yet thin
enough to bend to the shape of whatever I'm stepping on. So when I'm braking around a
sharp turn, or hitting the gas to avoid a big semi, my All Stars keep me connected with the car,
and with the road." Other chucks wearers tell us that chucks are great for playing the drums.
With your left foot on the hi-hat pedal and the right foot on the bass drum pedal, the flexible
sole of your chucks make you feel as one with your drum set. Another chucks wearer reports
that chucks are great secondary footwear on hiking or cave exploration trips. After arriving at
the location, he takes off his heavy hiking boots and puts on a well broken-in pair of high-tops,
because it is so much easier to crawl around and explore wearing chucks.

7 **Chucks epitomize retro appeal.** An interesting develop-ment in recent years has been the growth of the "retro" footwear market. Turned off by the increasing high technology and expensive prices of high performance sneakers, people are choosing to wear classic models of shoes made by Con-verse, adidas, and Puma instead. Retro shoes are popular because they have the look and style that people remember fondly and want to wear again. People into the retro look are rebelling against what they consider to be pretentious about today's overly commercial athletic shoe market, preferring to dress in shoes that represent a more uncomplicated time.

1990s catalog photo of classic retro chucks.

8 **Chucks represent simplicity.** One of the best features of the Converse Chuck Tay-lor All Star sneaker is its simplicity of design, aptly described in an advertising campaign as "just a piece of rubber and a blank canvas." For some people, this simplicity is the essence of why chucks are considered "cool" footwear. For others this simplicity is more "down home":

The classic white high-top is just a "piece of rubber and a blank canvas."

Chucks in a store.

chucks are friendly, comfortable footwear, and wearing them is a basic pleasure of life.

9 **The price is reasonable.** At first, chucks were considered expensive; they were the premier basketball shoe of the day and you had to pay for the privilege of wearing them. I remember that my first pair of black low-cuts, purchased in 1964, cost an astronomical $9.95, double the price of other athletic shoes, and my mother was shocked that I didn't bring back any change from the ten-dollar bill she gave me. But this perception changed in the next three decades, starting in the 1970s, when the price of a pair ranged from twenty to thirty-two dollars, while the new high performance shoes ranged in price from sixty to two hundred dollars. Now chucks were an inexpensive bargain. For the price of one pair of expensive Air Jordans, you could buy five pairs of chucks, and in different colors as well. Chucks were very popular among college undergraduates for their "student price." These days, chucks are priced above the middle price range, as of

★ ★

Levi's ad showing chucks.

this writing retailing for about fifty-five dollars for core models, sixty dollars for seasonal colors and prints, eighty-five dollars for the premium All Star 70, and well into the one-hundred-dollar range for designer models like those made by John Varvatos. Now, the consumer is paying for fashion again. Luckily for Converse, chucks are considered fashionable so people are willing to pay more these days for their pairs of chucks.

10 Chucks are the same yet different.

The look of a pair of chucks is distinctive, yet there are so many different ways you can express yourself by the way that you wear them. Some people choose to keep their chucks in immaculate condition, cleaning off any dirt after daily wear and making sure that the laces are kept flat and untwisted. Former Columbus, Indiana, high school basketball coach Bill Stearman described it this way: "When I was wearing them, it was a great pleasure to have a new pair of Converse shoes. You took care of them just like you took care of an automobile." Other people prefer the well-worn look and get their chucks dirtied up as quickly as possible. The way you lace up your chucks makes a statement. Some people like them laced up to the top; others like them laced up only part of the way. Some people like the canvas of their high-tops worn folded over, while others wear them the traditional way. Some people like the tongues of the shoes folded out instead of held under the laces. There is also a long tradition of making a statement with the shoelaces themselves on a pair of chucks by replacing the standard white laces with something else. Today, shoelaces for chucks are available in dozens of

Chucks with neon laces.

regular or bright neon colors; in flat, narrow, round, retro, or fat widths; or in multicolor weaves. You can also buy reversible shoelaces with two colors or fat laces with printed images like skulls, checkers, or stars. Shoelace choices too confusing? Now some slip-on models of chucks have no laces at all. They are held together by hidden elastic strips connected to the canvas uppers and the tongue.

11

Chucks have great variety. No other shoe comes in so many colors, patterns, and styles as the Chuck Taylor All Star. Chucks fall into two categories: the

Pairs of chucks laced up in a variety of different shoelaces.

★

31

Chucks go to the prom.

core models of classic high-top and low-cut black, red, navy blue, and white canvas, which are always available, and seasonal models, usually only made once, which come in bright and unusual colors and a variety of canvas patterns. Seasonal chucks come in high-top, low-cut, knee-high, and slip-on models. Seasonal chucks can be made with special fabric or even leather uppers. Seasonal chucks often have special features like multicolored canvas uppers, unique drawings or pictures, double tongues (in double colors), a worn or distressed look, or a foldover (roll-down) design. It is now even possible to design your own special pair. Whatever it is that attracts you to chucks, you would have to agree that they make a statement. That is why you always notice someone wearing chucks in a crowd.

12 **Chucks are versatile.** Chucks can go with just about any style of clothing. Although chucks are no longer confined to the basketball court, they still look great with basketball jerseys and shorts, and other athletic sportswear. The classic casual outfit for chucks is a pair of jeans and a T-shirt or sweatshirt. This "look" has been officially recognized by Levi Strauss & Co., and chucks are often shown in ads for Levis. In warmer weather, chucks look good with shorts, worn these days with or without socks. Chucks are practical for outdoor water activities, on rocks and in streams and rivers, because they are flexible, protect your feet, and dry out quickly. Chucks look great with more dressy outfits for men, like sport shirts and Dockers or even with dress shirts, slacks, and ties. You see women wearing chucks with all kinds of activewear, pants, blouses, and dresses. People like their versatility and the familiarity that wearing them brings.

How chucks have touched people's lives

AT **THE CHUCKSCONNECTION,** we collect and preserve personal stories about the importance of chucks in people's lives. You can't buy or make up this kind of brand loyalty—it comes from the heart.

Abbott wedding party.

Going out on that first date? Forget the flowers and candy. Just remember to wear your best pair of chucks! Many women have described how they have fallen in love with men because they were wearing chucks, and just seemed so cool because of it. Beth Jones, a writer for the *Roanoke Times,* describes their allure this way: "Just as peahens are wooed by the large, colorful tail feathers of peacocks, I go weak in the knees for guys who wear Chuck Taylors. He can be as homely as the runner-up in a one-man ugly contest. He can still be living at home with his parents. He can want me to watch his favorite *Star Trek* episode. As long as there are All Stars on his feet, my standards go out the window. Lots of women suffer from this obsession with men who wear Chuck Taylors—a condition which I will refer to simply as 'the fever.'"

In some romances, chucks go with the happy couple directly to the altar. Cheryl Abbott describes the events leading up to her wedding, in which the entire party wore chucks: "Since we have gotten together, we have been in many weddings, and Doug is always complaining about his dress shoes being uncomfortable. Doug was in a wedding last August, and after the wedding was over, he changed into his Converse. Everyone at the reception made comments about them. I never realized how much people notice your shoes. Again this May he was in a wedding and did the same thing. Even when we attend weddings, he dresses up and wears his Converse. Everyone always comments. And yes, he did wear them when he proposed to me. He had just come in from his mom's house and got

Haddon wedding photo.

Kid getting first pair of chucks, from 1961 Converse yearbook.

down on one knee in the middle of our living room and proposed. So when we set our date and started making plans, I said to him that he could wear them through the whole wedding and reception if that is what he wanted. When we told our best man, Tyler, he said he would wear them, too, so he went out and bought his first pair. When Doug and I were talking about it one morning, he made the comment, 'Wouldn't it be great if we could get everyone in the wedding party to wear them?' So, I just said, 'Why don't we all wear them?'"

Charles Haddon describes how he wooed his future wife, Nancy, with pairs of chucks. "Every birthday and Christmas I would give her a pair of chucks along with different Converse apparel. When we finally visited friends and they saw her wearing chucks, they knew she was a keeper. As our relationship began to mature, I told her that I had purchased a pair of patent-leather chucks years ago in hope that I would wear them at my wedding if that were to ever happen. She immediately nixed that idea and said that she would never be involved in a wedding with sneakers as part of this solemn occasion.

Three generations of chucks in the Bill Storer family.

Do white high-tops make you a better person?

"After a period of time and thought she told me that if it would make me happy to wear chucks at our wedding, I could. Upon hearing this great news, I began my search for a pair of chucks for her to wear. I finally found a pair of jewel-leather chucks over the Internet. When I presented them to her and told her that it would make me happy if she would wear these so we could be a matching pair, she agreed. On December 29, 2000, we were wed, and the wearing of our chucks proved to be a great idea. Both family and friends commented about them and wanted an up-close look at them."

For many baby boomers, lacing up their first pair of real chucks was a defining moment in their lives. Back in the 1950s and 1960s, owning a pair of chucks represented your coming of age. "You were so proud to wear this shoe," said University of Utah basketball coach Rick Majerus in an interview with Jack Wilkinson of the *Atlanta Journal-Constitution*. "They were the Air Jordans of their day. It wasn't about style. It was about prestige. You gravitated to them. We were getting the same shoes as the pros." Wilkinson goes on to say, "You no longer wore Keds, or PF Flyers. You were no longer a kid. You were a man. A hoopster. You wore Cons."

Staff members James Whitmore and Robert Parker at Jefferson County Traditional Middle School like to wear black high-top chucks.

Bill Storer, now a forensic specialist, described what it was like before he got his first pair of chucks. "I wanted a pair as a fourteen-year-old so bad I could hardly think of anything else. Kids' prayers do get answered. I got hooked on my chucks the first time I laced on those magnificent, black, aromatic [made in] USA devils." Chucks then became an important part of his life as he came of age. "I was laced in my high-tops for a lot of 'firsts'—my driver's test, my first part-time job after school, my first real date, my first real kiss, and for my first real boxing match in college." Bill was wearing chucks when he learned to shoot a .22 caliber Colt pistol and when he shipped out to Navy boot camp. Later he went to college and graduated wearing them. "I still wear them every day in my lab."

Callie Kizziar describes how finally getting his own pair of chucks was an important event in the life of Joe Baustert. "Joe, from a lower-class

Everyone should have at least one pair of well-worn chucks.

country family, knew the impact of not owning a pair of chucks. For three years he watched as many kids his age were rising the popularity ladder by having a pair of chucks. He wanted to fit in so much that he once painted the All Star emblem on his TG&Y look-alikes.

"The only problem was that Joe painted Chip Taylor instead of Chuck Taylor. You can only imagine the embarrassment he endured. Finally, after selling many pop and beer bottles, Joe could afford his ever-so-desirable white Chuck Taylors. He now felt normal and knew that everyone else saw him that way. Today Joe realizes that chucks are just a fashion statement, but in his youth he absolutely believed they made him a better person."

Robert Parker, a middle school teacher in Louisville, Kentucky, tells us how wearing chucks to work helps him to bridge the generation gap. "Being laced in chucks opens the door for conversation among the students. Mostly the boys will comment on the chucks and ask questions about how many I own, favorite colors, styles, etc. Normally these boys wouldn't make conversation with me as the teacher, but my wearing chucks puts us on middle ground. The chucks have caused the students and their inquiring minds to discuss fashionable footwear. The students are easily amazed when I tell them I have about forty pairs of chucks in my collection. I'm not only known as a teacher on the school faculty by name, but as the teacher who wears all the chucks. It is like having a little claim to fame, being known as Mr. Converse!"

You don't normally associate the wearing of a pair of chucks with life and death issues until you hear a poignant story like this one: "I would like to start off by saying thank you for a smile that your chucks brought to us. My name is Larry and I am fifty years old. I wore chucks as a child—they were the shoe to wear. In growing up and raising a family, I found out that they would again come back to my life. I am a photographer and travel quite a bit. In returning home on one occasion, I stopped by a store and shopped for some clothes for my youngest boy, Scott, then fourteen, for his school year. I had picked out some other high-priced name-brand shoes and decided to pick up some black high-top chucks also. After getting home, I laid out his clothes, which he loved, and showed him the other shoes, which

★

made him happy. But when I brought out the chucks his happiness went to a glow, his smile really went to joy, which gave me the sense of doing the right thing to make this youngster happy. In August of last year Scott turned fifteen and proudly strutted in his chucks to school.

"On February 22, 2005, we lost Scott in an auto accident on his way to school, in which his brother, Philip, who was driving, was severely burned. When I arrived at the scene of the accident and saw my son lying there on the ground, he was covered up, but his chucks were showing. This scene is marked in my mind and I will never forget it. He was so proud of these chucks. When it came time to make funeral arrangements for this little boy I have been so fond of, I made sure that when he was buried, his chucks were on him. In honor of Scott, all of his friends who were pallbearers (about twelve of them) wore chucks."

chapter two

A Brief History of the Converse Chuck Taylor All Star Basketball Shoe

WHERE DID THE Converse Chuck Taylor All Star basketball shoe come from? The Converse Rubber Shoe Company was started in 1908 by Marquis Converse to manufacture boots and galoshes. Eventually, to keep his workers busy on a year-round basis, Converse decided to add canvas-and-rubber shoes to his product line, and in 1917 he began making the Converse All Star. The first All Stars had a very different look from today's models, and were not meant to be just for basketball, although at this time basketball was becoming very popular as an indoor gymnasium sport. Other companies like Spaulding, the US Rubber Company, and Goodyear also made basketball shoes. Yet from all of this competition, the Converse All Star gradually emerged as the premier basketball shoe, preferred by coaches and players at all levels of competition. Why?

The original 1917-style (inset) chucks were reissued by Converse in 1997 (above). A rare photo of Chuck Taylor in an Akron Firestones basketball uniform (right).

It was because of the efforts of one man, Charles H. "Chuck" Taylor, who successfully advocated and promoted the Converse All Star throughout his life. Taylor loved basketball, first as a player and then later as a clinician and coach. No one person had more influence on the development of basketball in this country during those years. Taylor was ahead of his time in the methods he chose to advocate and promote the sport of basketball. He had the foresight to link each new development in the All Star line with improved play on the basketball court. Today we would call some of his methods "networking," "celebrity marketing," and "brand name recognition," as he sought out the best players and coaches of his day, personally brought them onto the Converse bandwagon, and got their endorsements for Chuck Taylor shoes. Because much of what he did was behind the scenes, Taylor remains a mystery man for many people. Was he a real person or a fictitious marketing name like Betty Crocker? Charles "Chuck" Taylor

was a real person who was responsible for making the All Star the finest and most desired basketball shoe of his day.

Chuck Taylor joined the staff of the Converse Rubber Shoe Company at their Chicago office in 1921 as a salesman, and later as a player/coach for the Converse All-Stars, the company's industrial-league basketball team. Starting in 1922 at North Carolina State University, Chuck Taylor tirelessly promoted the All Star all over America by crisscrossing the country giving free clinics at high schools and colleges on how to be a better basketball player. Although there was never any obligation, he let it be known during his clinics that to be a quality basketball player you had to have the right shoes, and Taylor always had a trunk full of Converse All Stars to distribute to players and local sporting-goods stores. In a typical year, he would travel fifty to sixty thousand miles and attend at least one basketball game per night during the season. Taylor took an interest at all levels of the game. "He was just as apt to show up at a small college contest as at the leading tournament or major clash of national interest."

★

Chuck Taylor traveled around with a trunk full of chucks.

Taylor worked with the management of the Converse Rubber Company to perfect the design and manufacture of the All Star. His innovations, sales expertise, and suggestions were significant enough that the management decided to add his name and signature to the product, and in the 1930s, the Converse All Star became the Converse Chuck Taylor All Star. After World War II the ankle patch was gradually changed to its current look, with the words "Converse Athletic Shoes, Chuck Taylor Model" replaced by "Converse All Star" printed in red on a white background, and the two words of his signature separated by a bright blue star instead of being printed on the star. This circular red, white, and blue ankle patch is one of the best-known and most enduring logos ever designed. Today, nearly four decades after his death, that ankle patch is still placed on millions of pairs of Converse All Star shoes manufactured each year.

Taylor also wielded a lot of influence on basketball by promoting high school, college, Olympic, and professional teams through the Converse Basketball Year Books, an annual publication started in 1922 that summarized the previous season. The yearbooks had articles about offensive or defensive strategies and successful teams written by prominent coaches and sportswriters, and any team that followed the criteria for submission could be included in the book. Starting in 1932, Taylor began picking the college All America basketball teams, based on balloting from leading coaches and sportswriters. The 1970 yearbook noted that "since this voting takes place at the conclusion of each season, rather than in the midst of any campaign, and because this voting exceeds, by far, any similar nationwide poll, Taylor's selections have always been regarded as the best in the field."

Taylor developed and perfected the art of getting coach endorsements for the All Star so that in his heyday of the 1950s and 1960s, virtually every basketball team in America wore Chuck Taylor shoes. From the start of Olympic competition in 1936 through the 1976 games, every United States Olympic basketball team (and many teams from other countries) wore the optical white high-top All Stars that Taylor designed for them. During World War II, Captain Charles "Chuck" Taylor coached regional Air Force basketball teams, considered an important morale booster for the troops, and chucks were standard service issue for basic training.

Chuck Taylor's diligent work continued to pay dividends for the Converse Rubber Company. His influence continued to be felt in all aspects of the game and he was often described as Converse's "basketball ambassador." By 1970, Converse employed eleven former coaches

★

or star players to give clinics and promote the shoes. In 1967, Taylor helped break the color barrier by hiring Earl Lloyd and later "Bunny" Levitt on the Converse staff.

After fifty years of work, Chuck Taylor was inducted into the Basketball Hall of Fame in April 1969, then passed away a short time later, in June. This truly marked the end of an era, and in the 1970s things began to change significantly in the world of basketball. Without the guiding hand of Chuck Taylor, the dominance of Converse in the world of basketball began to slip away. By the 1980s, other companies, led by Phil Knight and the Nike Corporation, began to dominate the basketball shoe industry, and now people were following the trends set by Michael Jordan instead of Chuck Taylor.

But changes in the world of basketball didn't mean the end was coming for the Chuck Taylor All Star. A whole new trend in footwear was starting in America, and it eventually influenced

Vintage ankle and heel patches, current ankle patch (above).
University of Connecticut basketball team (right).

the entire world. The baby boomer generation, growing up in the 1950s and 1960s wearing chucks and other athletic shoes, decided that they wanted to keep on wearing them as adults in the 1970s and 1980s. The athletic shoe industry gradually became the dominant player in the footwear industry, as people clamored for all types of running, training, basketball, and tennis shoes. While these shoes had definite sports applications, many people bought them because they were fashionable and comfortable to wear. A lot of these pairs never even went near a basketball court or field of play. People were now living more casual lifestyles and they wanted to wear comfortable clothes instead of dressing up.

In order to compete with other companies, and to meet the demand for new and innovative products, chucks now were made in many different colors. Instead of your two basic choices of black or white, you could buy a pair in different shades of blue, red, green, gray, tan, and even orange. These new color choices, and later other innovations like prints, patterns, unusual fabrics, and special models for kids, teenagers, and young adults, helped solidify the role of the Chuck Taylor All Star as a fun casual shoe, and a shoe that you could wear to show your individuality.

The management of Converse had a tough time adapting to the 1980s. With the Chuck Taylor All Star no longer being considered a serious basketball shoe, the company seemed to be somewhat adrift as it tried to compete with rivals Nike, adidas, and Reebok. To compete in the new world of high-tech running and basketball shoes, you had to have some sort of a gimmick, like an air cell, liquid gel, special cushion lining, or pump. These new technologies were expensive to create and required a lot of investment capital that Converse wasn't used to spending. They spent a lot of money on a biomechanics lab to develop running shoe technologies, but the resulting "Energy Wave" running shoes never were very successful in the marketplace.

Converse also missed out on some market opportunities for chucks that could have revived their fortunes. When skateboarding first became popular in the early 1980s, many of the skateboarders chose to wear high-top chucks. (The film *Thrashin'* is a great example—more than thirty different characters wear high-top chucks.) But Converse didn't get heavily involved in this market with endorsements and new specific skateboarder products, so companies like Vans were able to take over and dominate that market, just as Nike did in basketball. Other extreme sports like BMX bicycling also had marketing potential, as you see "Cru" Jones and his rival Bart Taylor wearing black high-tops in the movie *Rad*. But you had to have the vision and personal interest to see the potential of these then-fledgling trends. Most of these extreme sports had their roots in California, where the New England–based Converse management had very little presence.

"Made in USA" chucks were embraced by the counterculture as an alternative to expensive leather high-performance shoes made in Asia by sweatshop labor. They became popular with musicians in rock bands, disaffected youth, yuppies, and vegetarians (no animal products used to make a canvas-and-rubber shoe!). They went through cycles of recurring popularity, as new generations discovered them and declared chucks fashionable again. They were also becoming a shoe of nostalgia—nothing said 1950s or '60s like a pair of chucks. Converse began to cater to this market, and new models of chucks were issued in response to the fashion trends of the season rather than the demands of athletes. Kathy Button-Bell, Converse's director of marketing in the 1990s, told the *Wall Street Journal*, "We want to disassociate the All Star from our basketball shoes and bring it into life in our [television] spots as a fashion statement." Rick Burton, director of the Warsaw Sports Marketing Center at the University of Oregon's College of Business in Eugene, described the trend this way: "Chucks got repositioned from being an athletic shoe to a fashion shoe to a counterculture shoe, and fashion is a tough position for an athletic shoe manufacturer." Without new sports or leisure activity tie-ins to broaden their potential market appeal to consumers, chucks were now relegated to a niche market for sales.

In the 1990s, Converse Inc. suffered a series of business losses, partly due to bad acquisition deals that lost money, financial misconduct by a few employees, endorsement deals with basketball players Magic Johnson, Latrelle Sprewell, and Dennis Rodman that ended up hurting the company rather than building sales of

Converse ad showing core models.

their new high performance shoes, and an attitude at the top management that took for granted one of their most important income bases, the mainstream user who still liked wearing the traditional Chuck Taylor All Star. Advertising for chucks was confined to the "MTV market" and designed to be "edgy and provocative." Converse advertising agency spokesman Rich Herstek described it this way: "These types of ads are what people in our target market are looking for. They aren't meant to appeal to the mainstream. Our customers have a higher shock threshold than others." Emphasis was placed on new lines of high-performance basketball shoes, many of which lost money. Inventories of chucks were sometimes shipped overseas creating supply problems with large customers like department stores and chain shoe stores. As a result, out went the chucks, and in came the Skechers and Vans.

Converse management also had trouble coming up with a consistent Internet policy for its retailers and never grasped the potential for sales of the Chuck Taylor shoe on the Internet. The country was in the middle of an economic boom, but Converse continued to lose money. By the turn of the century Converse Inc. was in dire financial trouble, and in January 2001, declared bankruptcy. The main American Converse manufacturing plant in Lumberton, North Carolina, was closed forever, with the last pairs of "Made in USA" chucks coming out in March 2001. The assets of the company were purchased later

that year by Cason and Simon, the Footwear Acquisition Company based in Santa Barbara, California.

The new ownership, unburdened by the huge debt built up in the 1990s, began concentrating on rebuilding the brand name of Converse, and their inventory of Chuck Taylor shoes and other models that had success. They kept the name Converse but moved the company headquarters to North Andover, Massachusetts. All shoes were now made in Asian factories in Indonesia, Vietnam, and China. The new management, under the direction of CEO Jack Boys, focused on a three-part campaign to rebuild Converse sales. The first stage was to reestablish the supply of their timeless best-selling core models of the Chuck Taylor All Star like the classic black high-top and low-cut.

The Triumph band backstage (above).
Skateboarders wearing chucks (left).

"Converse used to sell three times the canvas shoes it does now," Boys said in a June 2001 interview with Andy Murray of the New Hampshire *Eagle-Tribune*. The second stage was to build on the All Star line by creating new models and variations. "Maybe it's a combination of canvas and suede; maybe it's a new slip-on style. Once you own this shoe, you can do all kinds of variations," Mr. Boys continued. The third stage has been a return to making high-performance basketball shoes, trying to develop a modern-era equivalent to the Chuck Taylor All Star with their NBA endorser, Dwayne Wade.

★

Chucks appeal to the counterculture. It's fitting that the "phoenix of footwear" has a "flames" model.

The new emphasis on the Chuck Taylor line of sneakers was a resounding success. Chucks were back in the stores, and sales continued to rise every year. A whole new generation of young kids and teenagers, especially teenage girls, have become enamored with chucks. You also see a lot more adults of all ages wearing them. There are so many new models and styles it is hard to keep track of them all (as you will see in the next chapter!).

Seeing this new trend and realizing that chucks occupied an important portion of the athletic shoe market, Nike Inc. acquired Converse in 2003. There were concerns expressed at that time, as many chucks fans thought of their shoes as the "anti-Nike." To Nike's credit, they allowed the Converse company to stay on its course. The result was continued sales success for Converse and a big increase in Nike's profit margin.

Chucks are the phoenix of footwear. Just when you think they have crashed and burned and their run of success is over, they are reborn into the next generation with a new wave of popularity and enthusiasm. This has happened so many times now that chucks are acknowledged to be part of our mainstream fashion culture.

The Evolution of Chucks

1917 model All Star. Not a lot of resemblance to the Chuck Taylor All Star.

A 1931 advertisement shows the all-black All Star. Note that the shoes have ten pairs of lacing eyelets, but none for ventilation. In 1932, Chuck Taylor's signature was added to the ankle patch.

This 1936 ad shows the new Olympic All Star, an all-white model with red and blue trim. Chuck Taylor's name has now been added to the product line, which includes a black canvas and black leather high-top.

★

This postwar ad from 1946 touts the All Star as America's No. 1 basketball shoe. Although the shoe is still all black, there are several important changes. For the first time you see it shown with the proto-type of the modern ankle patch, laced in white shoelaces, and two ventilation eyelets are placed in the inside outer wrap of the shoe.

In 1948, the black canvas high-top was given a new brighter look, as the all-black outer wrap and toe cap was replaced with white rubber and black piping. The double rows of stitching around the eyelets are now sewn with white thread. The modern black Chuck Taylor high-top is born.

In 1952, the ankle patch shows a blue star for the first time. The shoes are shown with red laces, although they continued to come with white laces.

★ ★

This 1957 ad shows the introduction of the low-cut oxford Chuck Taylor, the newest member of the All Star family. Touted as a completely new conception in design incorporating features never offered before in a low-cut shoe, All Star low-cuts have an angle-cut high front quarter to provide wrinkle-free snug instep support; contour-fitted heel counters to assure glove-smooth, positive fit; and a seamless forepart to eliminate chafing. One important difference from today's low-cut models is that there is no "All Star" cloth patch sewn into the tongue.

This 1966 ad shows the introduction of the single star and license plate logo. First ad that shows the shoes from an actual photograph, and you can see a little of the black or blue heel patch. The ventilation eyelets are moving up onto the red piping. For the first time you see the rounded stitching for the inner canvas piece that was part of the manufacture until the late 1980s.

This 1973 ad shows the inside patch view of a red high-top for the first time. Chucks were now available in ten team colors.

1974 ad showing different models of chucks and one stars being worn. The ad touts that eight out of ten players still wear all stars.

1980s black high-top. Note the changes in piping and ventilation eyelet placement.

1990s black high-top. A lot of cost-cutting measures. Shorter flat shoelaces instead of the tubular ones. Stitching is changed and the extra canvas piece inside is eliminated.

Late 1990s black high-top. ID label is added, front stitching is modified.

Early 2003 black high-top, made in Vietnam, has Converse logo tag inside each shoe. Note differences in toe cap and piping.

2005 black high-top, made in China. This is what you see in stores today. The outer soles are now made with a rubber/textile blend. Chucks are manufactured also in Indonesia and Vietnam. In 2014, Converse changed the look of the heel patch, adding the word Converse to it (see page 2).

★

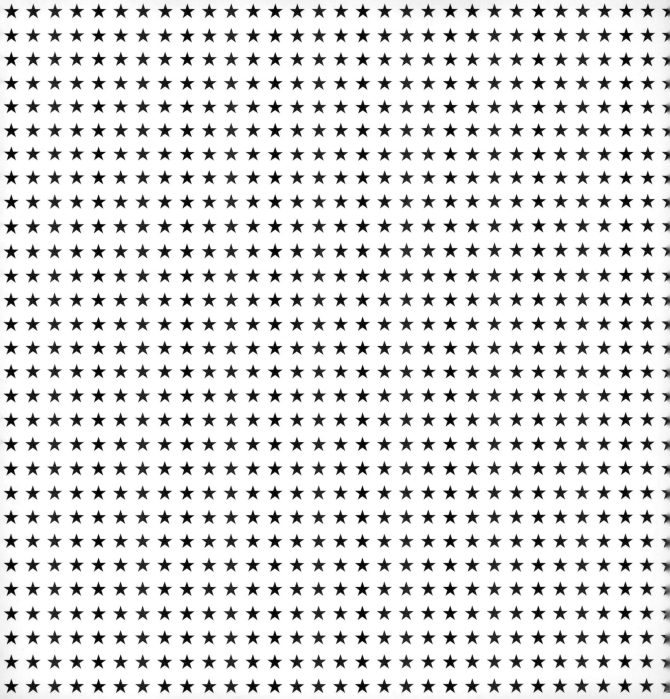

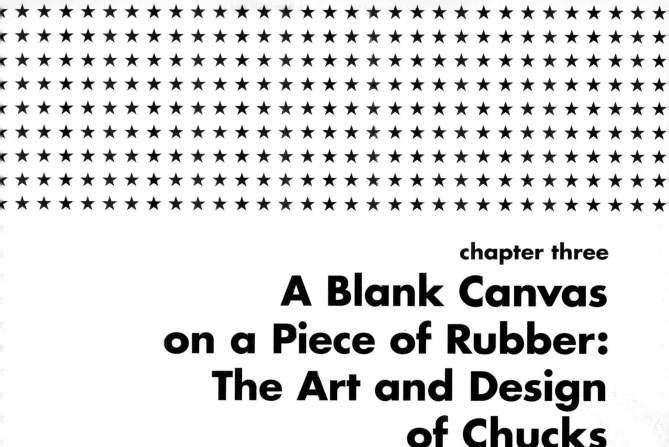

chapter three

A Blank Canvas on a Piece of Rubber: The Art and Design of Chucks

One Shoe, Many Ways

ONE WOULD THINK that a discussion of a canvas sneaker would be rather simple. But in the case of Chuck Taylor All Stars, there is really a lot of detail and depth to the conversation, because of all the different variations on the shoe that have been manufactured over the years. Chucks fall into two basic categories: the core color models that are in continuous production and seasonal models that are made in one-time batches and are usually available for about one year (or until they sell out).

Core models are the classic-looking chucks that have been available for decades and that represent the basic look of the product. Core chucks today are the black-and-white classic, all-black monochrome, optical white, natural white, navy blue, charcoal gray, red, and pink models. In previous decades, maroon, flint khaki, and pine green were considered core colors. Gray, always a popular seasonal color, was added in the last decade. Pink wasn't considered a core color in the past, but has become one today due to the greatly expanded popularity of chucks among girls and women.

The Classic Black High-Top

THIS IS THE most popular athletic shoe of all time, and the still the most popular model of all Chuck Taylor shoes made today. The shoe has been available for sale in pretty much its current version since the late 1940s. Black-and-white chucks were introduced around the time that the National Basketball League and the Basketball Association of America merged to form the National Basketball Association and begin the modern era of basketball. It was time for a new look, and their striking black-and-white appearance was very eye catching. Their appearance still has wide appeal today and they continue to be Converse's bestselling model of Chuck Taylor shoes. They also are popular in the visual and print media. Black high-tops appear in approximately 64 percent of all films and television shows that feature actors wearing chucks. Black high-tops appear in over 60 percent of all films and television shows that feature actors wearing chucks. If you combine the film appearances of black low-cuts with those of black high-tops, the percentage increases to nearly 75 percent.

The Optical White High-Top

THIS SHOE WAS designed for use in the 1936 Olympics in Berlin and made available to the general public in the year 1937. The Olympic All Star featured a real "Americana" look, with white canvas uppers and foxing contrasted with red and blue piping. In the 1950s, the shoe was brightened with the use of white dyes and the red, white, and blue ankle patch. The product name was changed to optical white. In those days, Chuck Taylor high-tops were the premier shoes for basketball teams, who could choose between wearing black or white high-tops. Optical white high-tops were Chuck Taylor's personal favorite, and one of the pairs he wore now resides in the Smithsonian.

Thomas sports a new pair of optical white high-tops.

The Red High-Top

THESE **BRIGHT RED** and white shoes with black piping are very much noticed by others when you lace up a pair. They definitely make a statement when you wear them. More than one writer has called them "sexy red," because they believe they have greater appeal to the opposite sex when they wear a pair. Red high-tops were featured in a television advertisement for Dodge with the slogan "Different." As the commercial began, you heard a voice talking at a company meeting while the camera pans along the floor showing a series of polished black dress shoes and suit pants. Finally the camera focuses on a brand-new pair of red Chuck Taylor high-tops and blue jeans as the voice says, "And now we will hear from our chairman. . . ."

Red high-top chucks . . . different.

In 2012, Converse announced that red core chucks would now become part of their Product Red line, meaning that a portion of the sale price would be donated to worthy causes.

The Navy Blue High-Top

THIS **MODEL FIRST** appeared in the late 1960s and are a common color alternative to black chucks. They blend in with jeans and look good with khaki or other light-colored clothing. Navy blue chucks are also distinguished from other core models by their all blue piping on the outer wrap, toe cap, and where the canvas joins the sole.

Lady car wash crew wearing navy blue high-tops (left).
Natural white high-tops (right).

The Natural (Unbleached) White High-Top

UNBLEACHED WHITE CHUCKS are popular with people who want a natural canvas-colored shoe, without the bright white dyes that are used to make optical white chucks. Except for their natural canvas upper and shoelaces, they are identical in appearance to optical white chucks.

The Monochrome Black High-Top

THE MONOCHROME BLACK high-top is the modern version of the original black All Star, which has been manufactured since the 1920s. Monochrome black chucks are completely black throughout, including the toe cap, outer foxing, outer soles, eyelet holes, and shoelaces. Currently, the ankle patch and heel patch are all black and made of embossed black rubber. If you look through the Converse Basketball Yearbooks, the mostly black canvas high-top

Inside patch view of a left monochrome black high-top.

and its leather partner were Converse's main All Star issues until the introduction of the Olympic white model in 1936 and the black-and-white model in 1948. The monochrome look has seen a resurge in popularity in the last fifteen years, and many recent seasonal models in other colors have been designed with all or part of the monochrome look.

The Pink High-Top

PINK CHUCKS WERE long considered a seasonal model, although they have always maintained the look of a core model. Over the past couple of decades, pink chucks have become more popular than ever with women, and now Converse lists them in their catalogues as a core color. Like red chucks, pink high-tops have always come with black piping. There have been many variations in coloring for pink chucks over the years, including a light (pale) pink model; neon pink, which has a bright raspberry quality to it; peach; and the standard medium pink, which has now achieved core status. Neon pink has been a very popular second color for two-tone chucks and various monochrome black seasonal models.

Inside patch and sole views of pink high-tops.

Core Low-Cut Models

ALL CORE COLOR Chuck Taylor shoes are available in low-cut (or oxford) models. The main difference in the way they look is that the canvas uppers are cut off just below the ankle, eliminating a pair of eyelets, and the inside ankle patch,

which is replaced with a rectangular cloth All Star "license plate" logo sewn onto the top of the tongue. Low-cuts were introduced as a more casual alternative to high-top chucks in 1957. The advertising for All Star Oxfords describes them as "a completely new conception in design incorporating features never offered before in a low-cut shoe." Features of the All Star low-cuts included an "angle-cut high front quarter to provide wrinkle-free snug instep support," a "contour fitted heel counter to assure glove-smooth, positive fit," and a "seamless forepart [which] eliminates chafing." One important difference from today was the lack of the square "All Star" cloth patch sewn into the tongue.

Seasonal Chucks

SEASONAL MODELS OF chucks made over the years come in all kinds of categories: single-color chucks, chucks with unusual features, and chucks with print pattern uppers. One way that you can tell seasonal chucks from core chucks is in the stitching you see in the canvas uppers. Seasonal models usually use only one color thread, while core models use white thread in the double rows of stitches that surround the eyelets and thread that matches the color of the upper on the ankle support piece. If you see a seasonal pair with both colors of stitching, there is a good chance that it is being considered for core status. Recent colors falling into this category included chocolate brown and charcoal gray. Charcoal received core status while chocolate didn't. A piece of advice: If you see a seasonal model that you like, buy it right away. You may never get a second chance!

Collage of core low-cut models (left).

Single Color Seasonal Chucks

AS AN ALTERNATIVE to the normal black, blue, white, or red core models, the canvas uppers for seasonal models typically come in bright or unusual colors, designed for summer or casual wear. They typically come in lighter shades of blue, purple, green, orange, yellow, and alternative tints of red and grey. Gib Ford, the president of Converse in the early 1990s, described the colorization of chucks this way: "If Chuck Taylor knew, he'd roll over in his grave."

2015 fresh colors low-cut chucks. Clockwise from upper left: jungle green, vibrant orange, pink paper, sapphire blue, dolphin gray, citrus yellow, collard green, larkspur blue, periwinkle purple, poolside blue.

Rainbow of seasonal colored chucks. Clockwise from top: huckleberry blue, bisay blue, royal blue, Caribbean blue, rage purple, maroon, orange, sienna, chocolate, taupe, oil green, Celtic green (right).

Print Patterns

THE CANVAS UPPERS of a Chuck Taylor shoe are a perfect place for some artistic expression. As a result, many types of printed-pattern chucks have been manufactured over the years. Some of these patterns are designed for kids, like the popular Batman and Joker models, a letters-of-the-alphabet print, a tie-dye print, the "conosaur" (a dinosaur print), and various animal patterns including the dragon, giraffe, leopard, and zebra. For teens, Converse has issued skateboard, surfer, and tattoo prints. Since the 1980s, Converse has issued chucks

in a variety of camouflage patterns, mostly in brown and olive green combinations. Another very popular line has been the "Stars and Bars," an American flag pattern that has been remade almost every year since they first were released. Stars and Bars are a white shoe with red stripes on the outer canvas uppers and white stars on the blue tongue and ankle support. There have been several variations of Stars and Bars,

Collage of kid print patterns (above right). Bill Storer sports his Stars and Bars (left). Blue and black denim chucks (opposite top left). Blue graphic star denim chucks (opposite top right). Collage of geometric pattern chucks including checkers, candy stripe, diamonds, and criscross (right).

Green, blue, desert brown, and faded camouflage high tops.

Stars 'n' Bars high and low, Puerto Rican frog, navy bunting, and destroyed flag.

Flames graphic prints on high top and low cut black chucks.

Tropical, Hawaiian, and surf pattern prints.

Multiple views of grafitti print and Converse Century high tops.

Converse logo and Sailor Jerry high tops.

Popular print pattern chucks.

a Puerto Rican flag foldover, a model with three times the stars and stripes, and even a "rummage" model.

Many of the pattern prints are geometric in design. These include the candy stripe, club print, or other combinations of stripes, checkers, crisscrosses, hearts, and snakeskin. Another popular print model was the flames graphic. First issued on black high-tops, flames graphics have also come in low-cuts and in a blue color variation. Other popular themes have been tropical and Hawaiian prints or those of a nautical nature like the "Sailor Jerry" line of high-tops. Over the years, Converse has issued a line of repeating logo prints featuring the All Star ankle or heel patch logo in a variety of combinations and colors. Most striking in appearance are the Converse Century line of chucks issued in 1907 to celebrate the hundredth anniversary of the Converse company.

Rock Band Tribute Chucks

As PART OF their Converse Century Project, the company began issuing models of chucks that pay tribute to specific rock-and-roll musicians or groups as well as the overall culture of rock. Some of these issues were part of their Product Red campaign of corporate giving. These shoes came with features appropriate for the honored band or artist. For example, in the case of the Ramones, a special distressed black high-top was released as a tribute to the classic rock band known for wearing well-worn pairs of chucks. The shoes have faded black canvas uppers with some tears and loose threading, pre-faded outer wrap and toe caps, and a scuffed and faded Chuck Taylor ankle patch like you see on distressed denim models. Special features include a Ramones-embroidered ankle patch on the outside of each shoe, and the word "Ramones" embroidered on the tongue of each shoe. The inner soles even have their slogan "Let's Go" printed on them. As a Product Red edition, the upper pair of eyelets on each shoe is red in color. The shoes come with natural laces, but as the outer wrap and toe caps were a perfect match, these sneakers were appropriately outfitted with hemp laces.

These sneaker issues came with special tags. The Black Sabbath tags describe them as a rock-and-roll original. One tag reads: "In 1908, Converse was born. Decades later, at the dawn of rock and roll, rebels, originals, hipsters, and hippies discovered sneakers as accessible and affordable symbols of everything rock and roll stood for. Converse sneakers have always been perfect for trips long, strange, and loud." A second tag talks specifically about Black Sabbath. "This legendary group from Birmingham, England, pioneered and defined heavy metal as a new musical genre. Their hard rock is dark and powerful, the first to mix the symbology of thunderstorms and church bells with epic power riffs and mesmerizing lyrics. The influence of their unforgettable legacy can be heard throughout the world in every modern metal band."

★
75

AC/DC Group Print   **AC/DC Switch**   **Black Sabbath Winged Graphic**

Volume 4   **The Clash Black High Top**   **The Clash Red High Top**

The Doors Logo Graphic   **The Doors Patches**   **Grateful Dead Tie Dye**

Grateful Dead Logo   **Green Day American Idiot**   **Green Day Kerplunk**

Jimi Hendrix Face

Jimi Hendrix Uniform

Kurt Cobain Doodles

Kurt Cobain Lyrics

Metallica Ride the Lightning

Metallica Graphic

Pink Floyd Prism

Pink Floyd Blue Print

The Ramones Product Red

The Ramones Black and Red

The Who Stitch Flag

The Who Flag Print

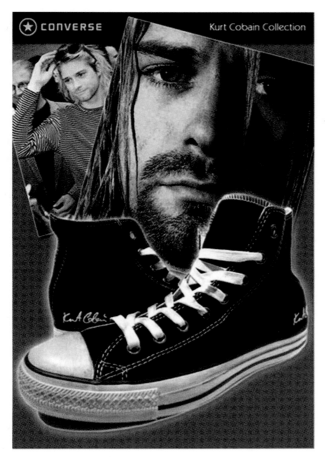

In memory of Kurt Cobain, Converse issued three high-top models. The Signature model has an embroidered signature on the outside uppers, a fabric ankle patch, and a pre-worn look on the rubber foxing and toe cap. The laces also have a worn look and are tubular like the original Converse laces. The insole has the slogan "punk rock means freedom." The Lyrics model is traditional black and white, with excerpts from different songs printed on the canvas uppers and on the inner soles. One other cool feature is writing on the inside of the white wrap—"Reward if found. K. Cobain." The white Doodles model has different sketches from Cobain's notebooks and the same reward inscription on the white outside wrap. For Van Morrison and the Doors, Converse issued a black-and-white high-top with black laces and The Doors logo on the outside, and an orange, tan, and brown patches high-top with black trim and laces and a graphic of Jim Morrison. AC/DC, The Clash, The Grateful Dead, Green Day, Jimi Hendrix, Pink Floyd, and The Who are also among the bands/artists honored with tribute chucks issues.

Comic-Book and Superhero Print Chucks

OVER THE YEARS, Converse has paid tribute to comic-book heroes with special print editions of chucks. The most models have been produced for Batman, along with The Joker. Superman follows with quite a few issues over the years. Bart Simpson, from the long-running animated television show The Simpsons, was recognized with a high-top print showing him writing "I will not waste chalk" on a blackboard. This is appropriate because Bart appears to be wearing blue high-top chucks in the series. The books of Dr. Seuss were also recognized with high-top and low-cut "Cat in the Hat" models of chucks.

Comic-book print chucks.

Distressed Chucks

THE **LOOK OF** a well-worn, perfectly broken-in pair of chucks has always been highly desired among its fans. "Distressed" models of chucks jump-start the process by starting with an aged look. The first models of shoes to be issued in this way were black-and-blue denim models released in 1999. The denim uppers were not sewn down at the edges, so the fabric of the shoes had a frayed look. The shoes had cracked and beaten-up Chuck Taylor ankle patches and were made with a gray-colored wrap instead of the usual white. And a final touch was the use of natural hemp shoelaces. A second variation on this was the graphic star line issued in 2003, which added a large printed star to the denim uppers. These shoes came in denim blue and natural white models. In 2005, Converse issued a distressed line of high-tops in red, black, and navy blue. These shoes have faded suede uppers with matching stitching and loose thread ends at the ankle support. They come with special classic laces featuring Chuck Taylor aglets.

With the changeover in manufacture from all-cotton duck canvas to a more synthetic "textile" upper, chucks are no longer able to wear down in the same way that "Made in USA" chucks did. The greater tensile strength of the upper makes it more likely to start separating at the outer wrap before it develops natural holes through regular wear. "Rummage" chucks addresses this issue by coming with built in holes in the uppers. Rummage chucks are also manufactured with outer soles and toe caps that appear to be worn down even when the shoes are brand new.

Rear view of distressed red chucks. (above).
Patches and rummage chucks (right).

Black Patches High-Top

Chocolate Patches Low

Black Rummage High-Top

White Patches High-Top

Stars 'n' Bars Rummage High-Top

Natural White Rummage Low

Another creative take on this idea was the "patchwork" model, in black and white, which added colorful patches to the holes on the uppers of the shoes.

Foldover (Rolldown) Chucks

FOLDOVERS ARE HIGH-TOP chucks with an inside and outside canvas color or pattern that can be worn two ways, as a regular laced-up high-top or with the top part of the canvas rolled over. These shoes have colored heel patches that match the overall color scheme, outer piping that matches the inner color, and outer stitching that matches the inner color. The shoes don't have a complete heel support piece in the back, which makes it easier to fold over the canvas. Foldover issues shown in the illustration starting at one o'clock and moving clockwise are black and green; red, white, and blue tricolor; black and red; navy and Carolina blue; red and gold; and navy, red, and gold.

Multicolor Chucks

MULTICOLOR CHUCKS WERE first manufactured in the 1980s, in tricolor models. Tricolor chucks had three different colors of canvas uppers, one on the outside, a second on the inside, and the third for the tongue and back ankle support piece. Some of the color combinations made were yellow-teal–salmon pink, green-red-purple, and green-maroon-black. Other versions of the tricolor used smaller patches of canvas sewn together and were released in red-white-blue and green-maroon-navy models. Some foldover models of chucks are made in three colors although most models are two-color chucks. (If you consider the white foxing and laces, they are tricolor!)

Circle of foldover chucks.

"Two-tone" chucks first came out as a seasonal model in 2003. Two colors of canvas are used for the uppers instead of one. The main color is on the outsides of the shoe, and the second color is both on the tongue and the heel support on the back of the shoe. Piping on the shoes is usually two colors along with the heel patches. Two-tone models have come in black-gold, black-pink, black-white, brown–Carolina blue, candy-cane red and white stripes, green-gold, gray-pink,

Green and gold two-tone chucks.

purple-gold, red-black, royal blue–orange, and royal blue–red color combinations. The black-pink two-tone was the most popular of these and was remade several times.

Knee-High Chucks

KNEE-HIGH CHUCKS were first made in the USA during the 1980s. They are an extra-high high-top shoe with twelve pairs of eyelets so you can lace all the way up to your knee. They also have a fold-down position, and extra snaps are placed on the sides of the shoe to hold the canvas in place when you lace in the fold-down position. The traditional side patch is placed higher on the shoe, and there is a smaller interior patch in each shoe that is revealed when it is folded down. Many of the models feature a pattern or alternate color interior. Knee-high chucks were revived in 2003 by Converse and have been made in both canvas and leather models, some based on the traditional knee-high and others emulating the monochrome look. They are mostly made in small batches and usually sell out quickly. They have also been marketed under the name X-Hi. Knee-high chucks are

**Sometimes I'm up.
Sometimes I'm down.
Today I can't decide.**

Introducing the Nechi™ All Star.™ From Converse.™ Available at fine stores everywhere. Ask for them today.

1980s Converse advertisement for knee-high chucks.

very popular in Europe, and more models are made for that market than for the US market. A few models are designed just to be worn in the knee-high position. As with the two-tone, models of the knee-high have been made in a wide variety of color combinations.

Uppers Made of Different Materials

OVER THE YEARS, seasonal chucks have come out in a variety of alternate upper materials besides canvas. These have included uppers made from gold or silver metallic fabric; a fur-like leopard pattern; embossed silk; corduroy; black, blue, and natural white denim; black and navy blue hemp; and a variety of woven plaid models. In 2008, Converse issued the "circuit board," a black high-top with a metal circuitry pattern glued to the canvas uppers, another quite unique creative design.

Leather is the most popular alternative material. These shoes either emulate canvas models, like a leather version of the classic black-and-white high-top, or are patterned after popular types of boots for hiking or other outdoor activities. The lines of leather chucks meant to serve as casual sneakers mostly come in black, brown, or white and have a monochromatic look, although occasionally you will find other colors like red,

Clockwise from left: Circuit board, iRobot leather, duck boot, chocolate hiker, and white monochrome leather (center).

blue, and green. One unusual line of leather chuck high-tops was the "jewel." These high-tops came in black or white glove leather and actually had the ankle patches on the outside of each upper instead of the inside. The patches weren't the usual glued-on rubber patches either. They were three-dimensional plastic patches with white plastic stars inside. These days you can get seasonal issues of duck boots, work boots, rain boots, hikers, and well-insulated winter boots, all made under the Chuck Taylor All Star name.

Special Designs

O CCASIONALLY **CONVERSE HAS** released creative variations on the Chuck Taylor shoe. The "cargo" was a high-top model available in khaki, navy, or olive green that had a special pocket compartment on the outside of shoe. The compartments, which were held together by a Velcro cover flap, could hold money, keys, or other small treasures. Many holiday or Christmastime models of chucks have been made in two tones or prints, but the most distinctive model was a red-and-green plaid high-top, made in the 1980s and 1990s. This model foreshadowed many of the new multicolor designs of this decade. Besides the bright red-and-green plaid uppers, the shoes had green-colored outer soles, green and red piping, a red heel patch, a special holiday ankle patch with a wreath surrounding the Chuck Taylor round logo, and a jingle bell attached to the ankle support piece with a red ribbon.

Gold and silver metallic and leopard chucks.

The "double tongue," first released in 2006, is a Chuck Taylor that comes with two tongues—one for lacing and the other for look. The bottom tongue, meant to be laced up all the way, has a rectangle All Star patch sewn on it, while the top tongue is meant to be worn folded down. The shoes come with two lengths of laces, and there is a shoelace slot in the upper tongue to help hold them in place. The shoes have a main outside color and two matching inner colors (like navy and light blue) on the inside and second tongue. The shoes can be worn as regular high-tops with both tongues laced up, or with one tongue folded over or rolled down. Double-tongue chucks continued to be a popular seasonal model, often made in bright prints and colors. Later, Converse made another variation on it, the multi-tongue low-cut.

★

Olive green cargo chucks (left). Black multi-tongue low-cut chucks (right).

"Simple details" takes the core chucks design and makes it bolder and more basic. Simple-details chucks were introduced in 2006 in black, red, royal blue, green, and pink high-top and low-cut models. The term "simple details" refers to the simpler construction and single color used throughout each shoe. These shoes are designed for and come with wide laces. The eyelet holes are bigger to accommodate wider laces and even the ventilation eyelets are of this larger size. The laces match the color of the shoe. The uppers are made of a heavy textile material very much like hemp. The texture of the uppers is a heavy, dotted-type of fabric. The ankle patch is much bigger than the traditional Chuck Taylor ankle patch and it is printed all in the basic color of each shoe. All the piping is also the same color, and the piping on the outer sole is a very wide, bold stripe. Even the word "Converse" printed in the inner sole is the same color as the upper of the shoe.

"Stencil chucks" were introduced in 2005. They were a fun kind of action shoe complete with a stencil kit that you could use to customize the shoes or paint the All Star license plate logo on other things. Instead of the Chuck Taylor key-chain tag, each pair came with a custom stencil kit in an envelope and a Converse "spray paint" tag that said, "Consider yourself tagged." The kit contained three small stencils along with some humorous directions. Stencil chucks were issued in black monochrome, white, and red high-top models, and black monochrome and pink low-cut models. The red and pink models have black toe caps and toe guards.

Simple details chucks.

Another special-design issue was the "Jackass" line of chucks, based on the MTV series and feature films starring Johnny Knoxville, who always wears black high-top chucks. The Jackass line included black leather, black canvas, and pink double-tongue high-top models, along with black canvas, black canvas slip on, and pink and black mini-skull- and crutches-patterned low-cut models. Except for the pink high-top, the shoes came with black laces, and each model has the Jackass skull and crutches logo on it somewhere.

"Multicultural" high-top chucks were a seasonal issue for 2006. There were three high-top models issued, plus a

Red-and-black high-top stencil chucks.

★
89

knee-high version of the parchment (natural white). The hibiscus-red and blueberry models were contrasted with parchment white, while the parchment (natural white) model had red, blue, and orange trim. Multicultural high-tops have unique stitching patterns on the canvas uppers, and the Chuck Taylor ankle patch is made entirely out of stitching. There are three rows of stitching under the eyelets and two rows above on the

Pink and plaid canvas high-top Jackass chucks.

canvas uppers, each in a different color and pattern that is meant to evoke the folklore of historic cultures. The canvas itself is of interest because each model has textured canvas uppers. The hibiscus and blueberry models are unusual because they have no piping strip where the canvas upper meets the rubber foxing; the parchment-white model has the same red-and-blue piping as the core white models.

With the popularity of its double-tongue issues, it was inevitable that Converse would come out with more "doubles" models. The "double upper," first released in 2007, has two canvas uppers, two sets of laces in contrasting colors, and two tongues. Available in high-top and low-cut, double-upper chucks come in plain canvas color combinations and plain canvas outer and print interior models. High-top models have two ankle patches, and some models have the All Star license plate logo on the tongues like low-cut models do. Two sets of shoelaces come with the double uppers in contrasting colors that match the uppers. The "layer-up" Chuck Taylor combined a high-top in one color with a low-cut in another

★

Multicultural high-top chucks (above).

variant of the double upper design. One more variation was the multiple upper high top. This shoe had five or six layers of thin canvas uppers. The uppers were rough-cut on their edges. Another intriguing line of doubles chucks were the "double-details" models, also issued in high-top and low-cut. These sneakers have twice as many metal eyelets, twice as many racing stripes along the outer foxing, and four rows of stitching on the uppers instead of the usual pairs. There are even four ventilation eyelets. Double-details chucks are a clever idea but a lot of work to lace up.

With denim jeans as a worldwide phenomenon and chucks being one of the best shoes to wear with jeans, it was no surprise that Converse would issue pairs of chucks with denim uppers. The stitched-details high-top was issued in a blue-and-black model, featuring elaborate stitching designs on the uppers like you would see on designer jeans. Along the lines of bling fashion have been issues of multiple-eyelet chucks, where dozens of eyelets were added to the uppers. Zipper chucks allow you to leave your chucks laced while you enter or exit them from the rear or side. A recent issue of zipper high-tops featured core colors with embroidered ankle patches. John Varvatos designs for chucks often combine zippers with suede uppers.

★

Black zipper high-tops and multiple-eyelet low-cut.

More special-design chucks.

The Converse All Star Chuck '70

IN **JANUARY OF** 2014, Converse released the Chuck '70 series of Chuck Taylor All Star athletic shoes, a line based on the manufacturing standards for chucks in the 1970s. This wasn't the first time that this had been done. In 2008, the Japanese Converse company issued an optical white high-top based on vintage standards, but this was the first time that a line of chucks based on vintage standards was produced for the US market. The exciting news about this new line of chucks is the restoration of many of the features that were taken out of the shoes starting in the late 1980s for the purpose of cutting costs. The advertising for the Chuck '70 line points out these restored features:

Probably the best thing about the Chuck '70 is the return to all rubber outer soles instead of the rubber/textile composite material that has been used lately. You notice the difference when you walk or run in a pair. Another difference between these shoes and the standard chucks sold today is in the toe caps. The black piping that defines the toe cap is inset more. This is because the outer foxing is about a half-inch taller, again like it

Diagram showing the features of the Chuck '70.

used to be. The natural line of the piping is separated from the diamond-patterned toe guard by a full half inch as opposed to the one-eighth inch in today's standard models. The piping

★
93

remains thinner, which looks fine. The foxing has also been slightly varnished, making the color more off-white in appearance. You can see the contrast between the foxing and the white laces in the photo. One other nice touch from the past is the return of the label area inside the tongue of the right shoe where you can write your name underneath the words "Converse Chuck Taylor Athletic Shoes." This reminds you that chucks were once the premier basketball shoe, and when you finally got a pair, you wanted to be sure not to lose them.

There are some misses in the design details. The shoelaces are narrower and less flexible than the ones issued with chucks in the 1970s and are much longer than needed. Providing extra long shoelaces is an unfortunately common practice on many Converse Chuck Taylor issues. This is especially noticeable because the lacing area between the eyelets is narrower than in regular pairs of chucks. Core models of chucks are sewn with a matching thread color to the uppers on the back spine lacing, not

THE CONVERSE ALL STAR CHUCK '70 SNEAKER

white thread like the Converse '70s have, and the ankle patches are not as bright. Despite these minor flaws, Converse is making an important step in the right direction with its Converse '70 line on the road to the restoration of Chuck Taylor All Stars to their full former glory.

You do pay for this extra quality, however. The high-top models are priced at eighty-five dollars and the low-cut oxfords at eighty dollars a pair. The first issues included the classic black high-top, a mustard yellow high-top, along with red, parchment white, and navy blue low-cut oxfords. Since then, other models have been issued in core colors or with print uppers. The shoes are made in Vietnam.

★

Chuck Taylor All Star II

IN **LATE JULY** of 2015, Converse introduced the Chuck Taylor All Star II, a new design for the classic sneaker. The shoes have these new features: a Lunarlon sock liner for more cushioning and arch support, a padded non-slip tongue for 360-degree comfort around the ankle and instep, a super soft micro-suede lining perforated for maximized comfort, and premium canvas for high-quality touch and texture. The shoes come in both high-top and low-top. The initial offering for the new line of sneakers was in four colors: black, salsa red, sodalite blue, and white.

There are a number of other differences between the Chuck Taylor All Star II and standard chucks, which received their last major design change for the classic black high-top in 1948, and the low-cut or oxford, which appeared in the mid-1950s. The new sneakers have matching shoelaces that appear to be 54 inches for high-tops and 45 inches for low-cuts. Ankle patches have single-color writing, blue on white for black, and black on white for salsa red, blue, and white models. The license plate patch on the tongue of each shoe for low-cut models features the same color combinations. All the stitching is the same color as the canvas, eliminating the contrasting color look of the original chucks.

Also absent is the colored racing stripe around the top of the outer foxing and the edge of the toe cap. The middle racing stripe is white, the same color as the outer foxing, so it appears more like an embossment. This is also true for the piping that accents where the canvas meets the rubber foxing and continues around the toe caps. This change is the most surprising, since the look of the toe caps and racing stripes is a centerpiece of Converse's lawsuits against other companies producing look-alike sneakers. It is significant that, although whited out, the racing stripes are still there. When double uppers and a few other

★

Chuck Taylor All Star II

seasonal models were first introduced, Converse did the same thing, but the vast majority of chucks issues in all kinds of seasonal styles and colors use mainly black, blue, or red racing stripes, which most people associate with the Chuck Taylor look. Most likely future issues will have colored racing stripes. Overall, this new look of single color uppers with matching shoelaces and all-white rubber toe caps and foxing tends to make the Chuck Taylor All Star II look like many of its competitors.

Converse management explains the reason for the new design as follows: "It all started with a simple idea: obsession. We obsessed creative spirits and realized they wanted more. A sneaker that meets the demands of their on-the-go lifestyle." It will be interesting to see how successful the new design will be and what kind of acceptance it will gain. The changes are significant, although this design stays truer to the traditional design than some of the recent variations we have seen. The last significant attempt at changing the design and appearance of the Chuck Taylor sneaker was in 1996, when the Converse company introduced the All Star 2000, which was a high-tech leather shoe designed to compete with Air Jordans. They only lasted about a year, as the consumers who wanted to buy chucks overwhelmingly preferred the traditional model. It makes you wonder why Converse didn't just add some of these new innovations like the sock liner and non-slip tongue to the classic models of the Chuck Taylor All Star.

Pricing is part of that answer. As of this writing, the new line of Chuck Taylor All Star II shoes are priced at seventy-five dollars for high-tops and seventy dollars for low-cuts.

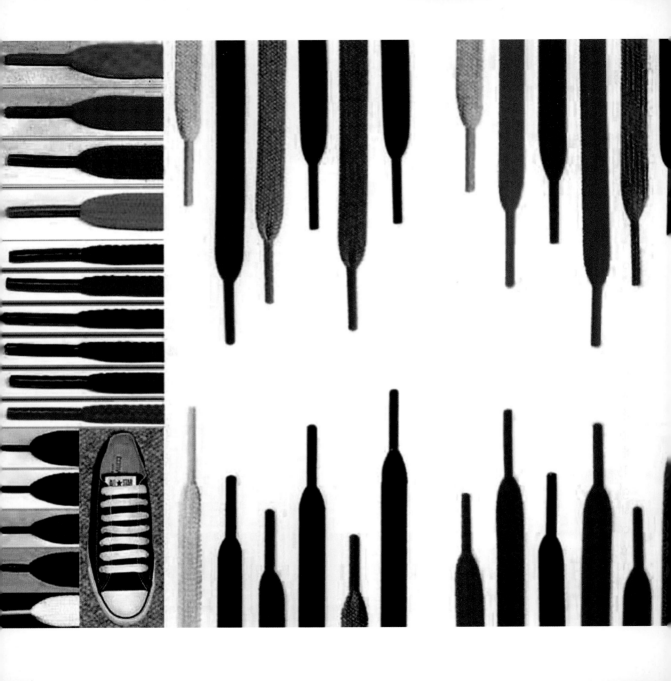

Customizing Your Chucks with Shoelaces

NO MATTER WHAT pair of chucks you end up with, you can still customize them further with different types and colors of shoelaces and how you choose to lace them up. Before chucks were manufactured in a variety of colors besides black or white, chucks wearers would often substitute different colored shoelaces to personalize their chucks. The laces could reflect team colors or just the desire to have a different look. This tradition is still very much alive today, with dozens of different colors available besides the typical flat, white athletic lace. The best athletic laces are the stretchable flat, tubular laces that came with every pair of chucks until around 1990 when they were replaced with ribbed single layer laces in a cost-cutting move. Beside the standard flat or tubular models, shoelaces now come in retro, fat, and extra-fat widths; in different weaves like rainbow or red, white, and blue; in narrow, round models like you see on many running shoes; in reversible two-color models; and in

Alternate lacing patterns for chucks.

★
99

print patterns with checkered squares, stars, skulls, or other symbols. So there are plenty of ways to express yourself.

How you actually lace up your chucks can be an important method of self-expression. Do you like them irregular and twisted or do you take time to straighten out the laces so they are not twisted? (They do last longer, look more consistent, and stay more securely tied the second way!) Do you lace with the string starting over or under the bottom set of eyelets? Do you like the over-under pattern or under-over as you lace them up? Some people like the straight-across lacing method, often used in advertising photos. This lacing method does not secure the shoe as well as the cross-eyelet lacing method. There are dozens of other lacing designs to make a statement with, as you can see in the illustration.

Design Your Own Chucks

IF YOU'RE STILL not satisfied with all of these choices, Converse has a program where you can actually design your own pair of chucks for as little as seventy-five dollars. First, you select whether you want a standard or print canvas

The details

■	Outside Body Color: **Black**
■	Inside Body Color: **Navy**
■	Heel Stripe Color: **Pine**
■	Tongue Color: **Red**
■	Lining Color: **Pine**
□	Rubber Sidewall Color: **White**
■	Racing Stripe Color: **Red**
□	Stitch Color: **White**
□	Lace Color: **White**

Design your own chucks, shoe details.

high-top or low-cut model shoe, or something more like a leather upper, side zipper, or even a Chuck '70. Then you choose the outside and inside colors along with the tongue and heel support colors from the available choices (you can create a four-color look if you so desire). Next you decide on what color of outer wrap, inner lining, piping, color stitching, eyelets, and shoelaces you want for the shoes. You can even add a personalized name or word on the heel support or outside canvas with your choice of color and font. After you complete your design, which can be saved if so desired, and pay for the shoes, it takes two to three weeks for delivery. With the design-your-own-chucks program, you can get a pair of chucks that is truly the perfect model for you. This is also a way to get certain hard-to-find pairs of chucks in seasonal or fresh colors and in half sizes.

Chucks as Art

JUST AS GREAT painters have created wonderful painting on canvas, there are artists who paint on chucks. The favorite model for this is the white high-top, but other models work as well. One artist who does intricate artwork on chucks is Laurie Lyden. She describes her work:

"I get my ideas for the designs on each pair of shoes based upon the person I am creating them for, and what their interests are. My 'Sistine Chapel' of sneakers is the two pairs of custom chucks I did for the fourteen-year-old

Grids of the different views of Ryan's chucks and Seth's chucks.

twin sons of my very best friend in the whole wide world. Seth and Ryan are truly outstanding kids, and their shoes are completely over the top. They're both into math and science. For Ryan's shoes, I went online and got the first two hundred or so digits of pi, and incorporated them into a grid pattern with a different color background for each number. The result was a nifty sort of random mosaic that I feel says something about the hidden beauty in numbers. For Seth, I looked at illustrations of the DNA double-helix molecule found in medical arti-

cles online, and created it in 3-D, with a caption that says, 'How do you spell DNA?' That was one of my first experiments in color blending on the shoes.

"They're both fans of the Star Wars series and the Douglas Adams's The Hitchhiker's Guide to the Galaxy series, and so those themes are present on the shoes. Each shoe also has a rock-and-roll side featuring bands that the boys are into. The figure-ground pattern is present on both pairs. The colors were inspired by their school colors. Each pair has their first and last names on the toe, in the space between the last set of eyelets and the rubber of the toe. There are also messages on the strips that run down backs, references that Douglas Adams fans would recognize. It took me about a month to do each pair."

Another example of chucks art (top). Chucks drawn with marking pen on rubber parts (bottom).

Chucks art doesn't have to be that extensive, and it doesn't have to be confined to the canvas uppers. A long-time tradition among chucks owners is to take a permanent marking pen and draw on the white outer foxing and toe caps of a pair of chucks. The white rubber is a great surface on which to draw and show some individual expression, if you are so inclined. Marking pen art can take the form of a personal graphic design, a short slogan, a name, or your own signature.

Due to the prevailing rock and popular music association with chucks, individuals and small businesses have created tribute artwork on pairs of chucks for their favorite bands and artists. Famous artists like Bruno Mars and Ed Sheeran have created personal artwork on chucks for charity auctions. Rapper Wiz Khalifa has collaborated with Converse on his own line of shoes that he designed. No other footwear provides so many options for self-expression as a pair of chucks does. It's quite amazing when you consider how this classic basketball shoe continues to reinvent itself in our popular culture.

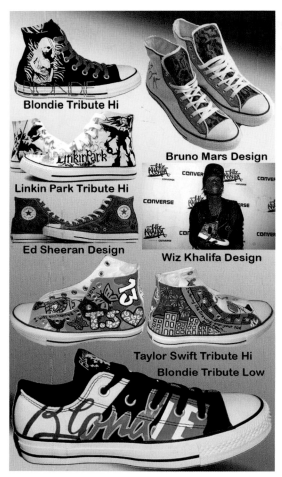

Blondie Tribute Hi

Linkin Park Tribute Hi

Ed Sheeran Design

Bruno Mars Design

Wiz Khalifa Design

Taylor Swift Tribute Hi
Blondie Tribute Low

Tribute and celebrity-designed chucks.

★

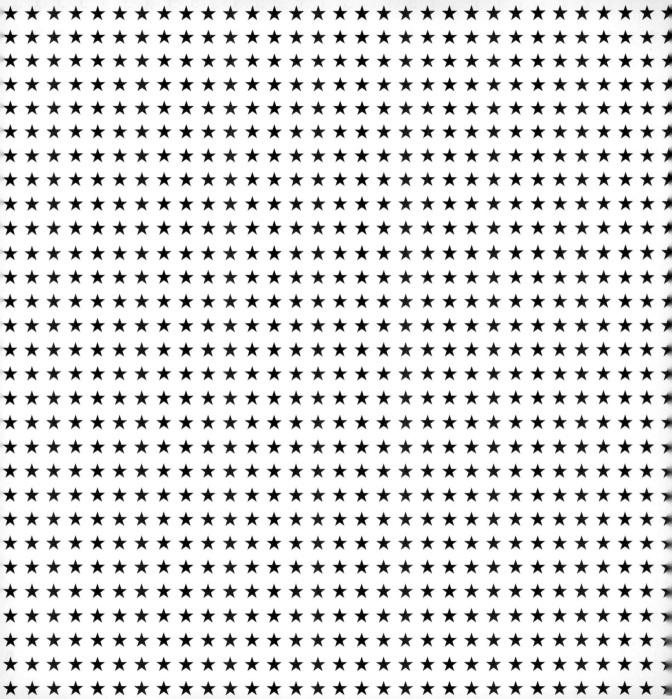

chapter four

The Marketing of Chucks

JUST AS THE history of the Chuck Taylor shoe is full of interesting twists and turns, their marketing has been different from the typical mass-manufactured product. One of the reasons for Converse's success over the years was due to the independently-owned local stores throughout the country that have specialized in selling chucks.

One of these dealers was Corky Fulton, who worked out of King's Mountain, North Carolina, a small town west of Charlotte. Fulton owned and operated ClassicSportsShoes.com, HomeRunExpress.com, BasicSkiwear.com, and SageSport.com, Internet businesses that specialized in athletic and outdoor footwear and clothing and gear, along with five retail stores in the Carolinas under the name SageSport. Typically, Fulton maintained a warehouse inventory of over ten thousand pairs of retro shoes, with sales of chucks representing about 25 percent of his business.

Corky Fulton working in his office.

Corky got his start dealing with athletic clothing by working for his father, who owned a department store in King's Mountain. In those days, the store sold Keds and the Converse Coach, a shoe nearly identical to the Chuck Taylor. Corky wanted to carry Chuck Taylor shoes at the store but wasn't allowed to do so, because you had to be a store with a sporting goods department to become a reseller. "For every pair of Coaches we sold, we could have sold twenty pairs of Chuck Taylors because they were the hottest athletic shoe available at that time. So one day, I went to the Wilson sporting goods company and purchased six tennis racquets and a machine that would restring them. Now our store had a bona fide sporting goods department and could carry the Converse Chuck Taylor All Star."

Sales of chucks took off and were helped by the fact that the main Converse factory had just been moved to Lumberton, North Carolina, a town that was only sixty miles away. "I could drive there in my pickup truck and get whatever we needed." In fact, one of the things that Corky liked the best about the company over the years was the fact that they maintained a replacement inventory of Chuck Taylor shoes at their factory distribution center, so sizes or models that sold out in between product orders could be easily replenished. In the early years, the store carried the four basic core colors of chucks and Jack Purcell tennis shoes.

In 1982, Fulton launched his first athletic clothing store under the name SageSport. The store was successful and he gradually added more stores in different locations. With the growing popularity of athletic footwear and clothing, Corky was soon carrying over a dozen different brands of shoes besides Converse. He began to notice some interesting things about the business. Pro models would usually sell well, but their sales could change very rapidly with the fortunes of the player who endorsed them. Most pro models were made on a one-time basis, like seasonal chucks. You were unlikely to get any fill-in sizes unless the shoes were made again. With the Chuck Taylor shoe, he noticed that they would sell in seven-year cycles. Some years they were in fashion and very popular, and he could hardly keep them on the shelves. In other years, people's interest in chucks would wane—they were considered out of fashion—and so sales would mainly be to dedicated wearers of the shoe.

Business methods in the athletic shoe industry changed quite a bit in the 1980s when Nike began to dominate the athletic shoe business. "They set up the idea that you should get the order first and then make the shoes. Instead of sales representatives coming around every three to four weeks to check on your inventory, you now had to place your orders three, six, or even nine months before they would be delivered." Once the orders were in, they were sent overseas to factories in Asia to be manufactured and delivered to the American market in large shipments. Whatever was in the shipments represented the total inventory for that particular product. Nike liked to create new models for every year, so it was unusual for the same product to have a long shelf life. Even their bestselling Air Jordan and Air Force models went through many design changes over the years. Eventually Converse switched over to the "order first, make the shoe second" practice, especially with the financial issues the company had in the 1990s. Sometimes items would be shown in the company's catalog, but would not be manufactured if there weren't enough pre-orders, a practice that still continues today. But core chucks were almost always available, were always manufactured every year, and always looked the same, so they continued to figure the most in the bottom line. Corky's wife, Barbara, who helped with the business, described it this way: "I liked restocking black high-tops and low-cuts on our warehouse shelves, because I knew they would soon be money in the bank."

In 1997, Corky launched his Internet businesses and watched as the growth of the Internet changed his whole business model. With the online store open 24/7 all over the country, people now had access to products in his inventory whenever they wanted. One of the problems with carrying chucks in a typical retail store was you normally couldn't afford to carry all of the models. You had to speculate how popular the seasonal models will be, due to the ordering procedure, so mostly you would choose to carry a limited, "safe" selection. With the Internet, your potential customer base is greatly expanded. Fulton found that he could carry almost the complete line of chucks made every year and keep most of the inventory right in the warehouse, because someone, somewhere would want to buy that orange-and-green high-top that might not move into a local store. Another successful program that helped bring customers to his online stores was links from affiliate websites. Affiliates added hundreds of additional "hits" each day into the online stores and received a commission for each sale that their links generated.

The Internet has changed the way people shop and buy shoes. "Before the Internet, people would go to the store, and if the product . . . wasn't available in the exact size or color they wanted, we could often sell them something similar. Now, nobody takes anything but their first choice because they can search the Internet and find it elsewhere." Credit cards have also changed how business was done. "Before credit cards, many customers would want to buy on credit, and have you bill them later," often causing a cash-flow problem. Now the credit card company handles everything, charging a fee to the merchant and interest to the consumer if they paid their bills over time, but the merchant received payment within a few days after completing the sale. The Internet allowed Corky and his staff to provide better customer service through emails that track the sales process from start to finish, and it was another useful resource beside the telephone for resolving customer issues or answering questions.

Another independent business is American Athletics, located in Charlotte, North Carolina. The store was started by Gary Church, who has had an interesting career selling athletic shoes. For many years, American Athletics was a successful running-shoe store in the SouthPark Mall, selling Nike, Asics, and other running shoes, along with clothing and gear for runners. He also sold Converse shoes. In the early days, he and his business partner would cover track meets and other running events, selling shoes out of their van at over thirty races a year. This was a good way to move inventory that would otherwise sit on the store shelves. "After I had the business there for seventeen years, the mall management told us that all the stores would be required to open seven days a week." This was too much for Gary, who has had a long commitment to his church and youth activities in the community.

"I spent the next two years looking around for a new business opportunity, trying other occupations out, but continuing to sell shoes out of my garage. Converse was the only company that would keep me in business without an actual store location. Part of the reason was that they were strapped for cash at the time and I had a track record selling Converse shoes. One day I had a conversation with two of my young employees, recent graduates from North Carolina State who convinced me that I needed a website." This was when online shopping was a very new idea, and Gary had no idea how things would work out. He decided to concentrate on selling Converse Chuck Taylors. When he contacted Converse Inc. about selling on the Internet, they were just setting up their first website, which was going to concentrate on the Dennis Rodman line of shoes. He talked to the webmaster who told him he could try selling anything out of the catalog. So Gary decided to try selling every model of Chuck Taylor that was

American Athletics staff.

being made. With the Converse factory nearby in Lumberton, he figured that he could take the orders that came in and then acquire what he needed from the factory to fill the orders.

Sales started very slowly, averaging just three to five pairs a week at first. Due to the cyclical nature of the business, some years he was lucky to sell one pair a day, while other years he would sell fifty pairs a week. But the business continued to grow, and eventually American Athletics was selling seventy-five pairs a day. He moved from a 1,500-square foot warehouse to a 3,000-square foot warehouse with around eleven thousand pairs in regular inventory. "We had so many different models that even the bathroom (which is very large) [was] used to store shoes." American Athletics has become a successful niche business on the Internet because they always try to stock pretty much every item that appears in the Converse catalog. This ends up being a service to Converse because they promote brand loyalty for dedicated chucks enthusiasts by having that hard-to-find item readily in stock.

"Right now, the black-and-white leather (iRobot) high-top is the bestseller outside of the core canvas shoes. And it looks nearly identical to the classic black-and-white canvas high-top. Designer chucks, like the John Varvatos models, have been doing well lately. It is funny to think of people spending 100 to 180 dollars for a pair of chucks, but we are moving three to five pairs of the different designer models a day." Having so many different and unusual models of chucks has resulted in some interesting sidelines for American Athletics, like their clown business. "Someone will call up and ask, 'Do you have a size seventeen pink high-top?' and I say, 'You wouldn't happen to be a clown, would you?' Our employees bust up laughing when they overhear the conversation." Even with all of their specialty models, core chucks still make up the majority of all sales. When asked why the classic chucks are still so popular, Church's answer is, "A pair of chucks gives kids their own identity," something that they never forget the rest of their lives.

★

Gary attributes his success to several things. One has been always working to provide great customer service. "We want to talk to our customers. We have always put our toll-free number right on our home page, instead of hiding it like other businesses do. Our customer base is very loyal. Out of every ten customers, six are new and four are returning." A second important factor has been the friendships that he has been able to cultivate within Converse Inc. A lot of the people who ended up in the corporate offices either worked in the factory at Lumberton or as sales reps in this area. This was important to his business in 1995, when the cash-strapped Converse management sold off nearly all of their Lumberton factory inventory to foreign affiliates because they paid cash in advance. In the United States this meant that there were six or seven months when core shoes weren't available. "Because of my connections within the company, I was allowed to pick up pairs (but only a hundred) of the very scarce canvas chucks a month during this time to maintain the brand loyalty. This helped to keep their most loyal customers in the brand during the lean times." A third important reason for success is Gary's propensity for moving out inventory that doesn't sell well. "I make sure my supply is clean and always sell off products that don't move after six months. Your first markdown is your best markdown. It is better to sell at a loss and reinvest in something that is selling. You will turn your money around and regain it back within the year, and you are not stuck with bad goods."

New black-and-white leather (iRobot) high-top chucks in their box.

With the success of Internet businesses like Classic Sports Shoes and American Athletics, along with the continually building presence of Internet shopping, the competition for sales greatly increased in the past decade. Larger sporting goods chains and department stores with hundreds of stores in malls across the country now competed for shoe sales on the Internet. They could get better wholesale pricing due to the huge size of their orders. Order discounts and free shipping started to become the norm. Larger companies could make up for smaller profits due to their volume of sales. Converse, who had initially not seen the potential in Internet sales, also got involved, often in head-to-head competition with its own resellers. Internet webmastering and advertising costs became a lot more expensive as Google and other online search engines changed their methodologies for listing websites. The search engine price for hits to keywords like "Converse All Star" tripled and quadrupled. Smaller businesses could not survive the razor-thin profit margins caused by these changes and the recession that hit businesses hard starting in December of 2007.

It was hard to reinforce the retail prices Converse set for its retailers when there was a lot of competition from small vendors on auction sites like eBay, who weren't authorized dealers but managed to get inventory. Converse responded to complaints about unfair competition by conducting their own review of all their dealers to make sure that all licensed dealers used their retail prices, which continued to edge up every year. The company promised to stop the discounted competition but has been unable accomplish this so far. As of this writing, eBay has over fifty-eight thousand listings for pairs of chucks on their website, most of them listing at around 25 percent off the retail price.

When asked about some of the current trends in the culture of Converse, Church has some interesting observations. "We have lost the glamour and vintage of the Chuck Taylor to progress. There is a whole new generation of people who just want to wear them as fashion.

★

Nobody cares any more about the past." One common wish from "purists" who decry any change at all to the original Chuck Taylor shoe is that Converse would revert to making a true classic Chuck Taylor shoe again, complete with aromatic vulcanized rubber, and all-cotton duck canvas uppers. "I really don't see this ever happening," Church says. "The manufacture of the shoes is a very complex process. The new methods and materials are here to stay. The shoes look more perfect now because of new automated production procedures, as opposed to the older methods at Lumberton where much of the assembly process was done by hand. You won't see a glue stripe on the canvas or unevenly attached toe guards on the new chucks due to the new processes." However it should be noted that Converse has continued to maintain the look of its core model Chuck Taylor basketball shoes, knowing full well the outcry that they would receive if they altered their basic appearance. And they have started to accommodate those who would like a return to older manufacturing standards with their new Chuck '70 line.

People who like wearing mismatched pairs help Internet sales.

Another trend that consumers have faced in the past fifteen years is the elimination of half sizes on most seasonal models. This was started because Journeys, the mall chain store that ran Converse's website when they restructured after bankruptcy, wanted to carry less store inventory for each model of shoe. "We have lost some business due to the even size-only trend," Gary tells us, "but Converse has been on the upswing lately, so we have made it back through greater sales." In the past few years, more of their seasonal issues have come in half sizes. This is due to the continuing popularity of chucks, consumer demand for half sizes, larger production quotas for a smaller number of issues each season, and the fact that Converse needs full lines of inventory for its own website, chain of outlet stores, and flagship retail stores in major cities.

Unusual items from American Athletics. Clockwise from top: green shamrock, blue/grey/white camouflage, military print, multicolor peace, eggs and bacon, maroon rolldown with plaid interior.

The sizing of chucks is one of the anomalies from the past that is still in effect today. Chucks have been made from the same outer sole molds for eighty years now. Each box of "Made in USA" chucks showed the size in four versions: USA men's, UK, European, and Japanese. The made-in-Asia boxes now show chucks in five sizes, adding USA women's to the list. The size number on the shoe's outer sole is the USA men's size. When chucks were originally made, the sizes were the same as other shoes in the stores. But today Converse chucks are the only shoes made using these original lasts and molds. All of the other companies have ceased to exist or have moved manufacturing over to Asia, where the sizes are smaller. Since virtually all of our footwear today is imported, the Asian sizes have become the norm, and now every dealer of chucks has some sort of size conversion table to try to fit your feet correctly based on this change in sizing. The best thing you can do as a consumer is be sure that your pair of chucks fits you correctly by trying them on. If you fit more comfortably in a half size, insist on it when you buy a core model. If you buy the wrong size over the Internet or at a store, you should be able to exchange your unworn pair for one that fits you better. An important part of the comfort you get wearing a pair of chucks comes from lacing up the correct size.

Gary Church of American Athletics.

In the new millennium, retail marketing continues to move away from the single-store businesses that support the brand to the large-chain stores occupying our malls and shopping areas throughout the country. A few smaller, family-owned businesses remain, like Sam's Clothing in Ann Arbor, Michigan, which has been selling chucks since 1946. Others are gone, like Jack's Shoes in Madison, Wisconsin, which recently closed after fifty years in business, or Corky Fulton's SageSport stores in North Carolina, which closed in 2014.

A mall store might only carry a few models of chucks, but with nearly fifty thousand malls and shopping centers nationwide, a mall chain with hundreds of stores is going to have more impact financially on the Converse company than the most loyal small business, even one that carries all of their product lines. "Sales of chucks will continue to occupy a niche market on the Internet," Gary explains, "and those companies that don't understand this will be sifted out the next time there is a business downturn." As we look into the future, where will the typical consumer go to buy a pair?

The Internet is clearly one place, as online sales continue to increase every year. To try on a pair of chucks, unless you live near one of those long-time stores that specialize in selling chucks, shopping malls with chain department stores, sporting goods stores, or athletic shoe stores are the place to go. And don't forget Converse's own national network of outlet stores and retail stores in major cities and thirty different states.

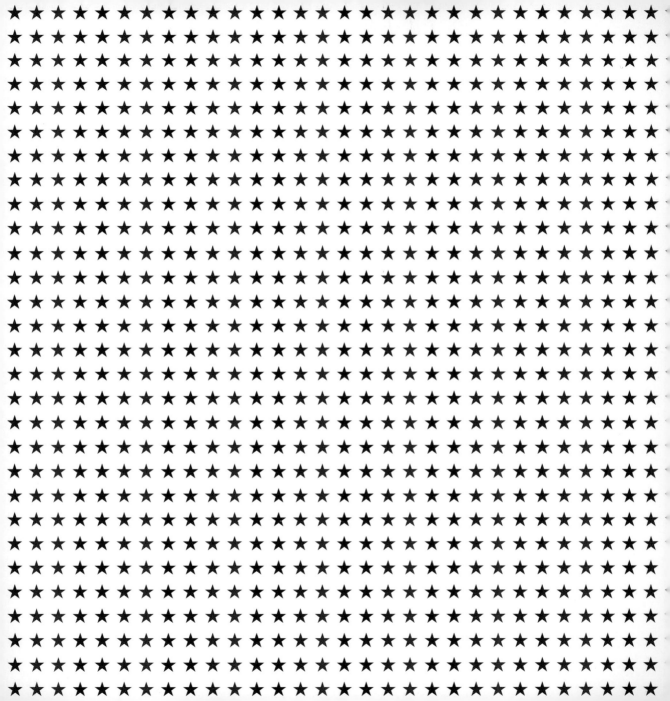

chapter five
Chucks in the Media

CHUCKS HAVE AN interesting presence in our media. Whether they become a subject for still photography, are worn by characters in films, music videos, or television shows, appear in stage productions, or are used in advertising, people tend to notice them. Occasionally, chucks even become part of a story line or song.

The Art of Photographing Chucks

BECAUSE THE LOOK of a pair of chucks is so unique and striking to the eye, they make an interesting photography subject. Black-and-white chucks are photographed the most, and there are several reasons for this. One is their popularity; the more you have of something, the more likely it is to be used, and black-and-white chucks still are the bestselling All Star. The design of the shoes themselves is another reason they photograph well. Most shoes are designed to blend in and not be noticed. Chucks are the opposite; their bold contrast of black and white is immediately eye catching. The white outer wrap sets off the bottom of the shoe, while the white double stitching on the canvas uppers sets off the outline of the shoe. The white toe caps and circular ankle patch are very distinctive in appearance. The thin lines of black piping help to define each part of the shoe. There are also the subtle features of the diamonds and other lines on the toe guards and outer soles. A black Chuck Taylor shoe will obviously photograph very well in black-and-white photography, and it brings that striking look of contrast into a color photograph.

After the black-and-white model, the next most eye-catching (and photographed) model is the core red high-top. Blue-, green-, and white-colored chucks are a little more difficult to shoot, as you have to be careful of how the lighting affects their actual coloration and you have less contrast to work with. Monochrome and seasonal models are the most difficult to photograph

Black high-top chucks.

due to the uniformity of a monochrome shoe and Converse's propensity these days for making most of their seasonal models without the white stitching on the front part of the canvas uppers.

You can find many photos of Chuck Taylor shoes on the Internet, especially on social media sites devoted to posting photos. Search on those sites using hashtags like #chucks, #chuck-taylor, or #converse. Or perform an image search on your web browser. Often, people take selfies of their chucks while they are wearing them with a cell phone or a camera. Here are a few suggestions to take better photos of your chucks. Be sure to switch to close-up mode on your camera. Your pictures will have a lot better clarity. Be careful of the lighting; it can change the coloration and shadows. On close-up shots, the flash may create bright spots. You might consider turning it off if you notice that happening. If you are shooting pictures of yourself, use the timer feature to get better-shot angles and poses. With a little practice, anyone can create interesting photos of chucks themselves.

★

The starting line of the LA Massacre in Thrashin' *(top left).*

Zack and his girlfriend, Jenny, go for a ride on Rip in The Skateboard Kid *(top right).*

The end of a fancy move in Back to the Future *(bottom).*

Films with Actors Wearing Chucks

WHAT DO ACTORS Tom Hanks, Brendan Frasier, Jeff Bridges, Jim Carrey, Josh Charles, Kieran Culkin, Jamie Lee Curtis, Zac Efron, Michael J. Fox, Edward Furlong, Leonardo DiCaprio, Dakota Fanning, Ethan Hawke, Josh Hutcherson, Logan Lerman, Justin Long, John Cusack, Emile Hirsch, Matthew McConaughey, Trevor Morgan, Keanu Reeves, Craig Sheffer, Christian Slater, Sylvester Stallone, Mike Myers, Chris Pine, Elijah Wood, Shailene Woodley, Michael Angarano, Anton Yelchin, and Arnold Schwarzenegger have in common? They have all starred in films wearing Chuck Taylor high-tops. On **The ChucksConnection** website, we have already documented over seven hundred films where actors in a leading or major supporting role have worn chucks. Although they don't list actors as product endorsers, Converse has done a good job of getting chucks out to them and costume designers for films.

Some cinematographers are especially good at including chucks in the way they frame their scenes, something we note in the film reviews featured on **The ChucksConnection**. Several skateboarding films are particularly good examples of this. *Thrashin'* (1986), *Gleaming the Cube* (1989), and *The Skateboard Kid* (1993) are full of great chucks scenes showing the main characters skateboarding. And there is that classic scene in *Back to the Future* (1985) where Marty (Michael J. Fox) fends off Biff and his cronies with an improvised skateboard. *Sin City* (2005), based on the comic-book characters of Frank Miller, was shot in film-noir style, black and white, but with a different spot color in each of the three main sequences. In the scenes with Dwight (Clive Owen), who wears red high-top chucks, the spot color is red. As a result, his chucks are often the only colored object you see in the scenes, a great visual

★
123

effect in the film as they stand out from the black-and-white scenery. In one great scene, Dwight escapes from a building by jumping off of a ledge, and the camera focuses on him and his red chucks as they float through the air and land on the ground. Elijah Wood also appears in the film wearing black high-top chucks in his role as Kevin, the silent and sadistic killer from the Rourke clan. His black high-top chucks look great in the black-and-white cinematography of the film noir genre. The best scene featuring them is the fight scene with Marv where Kevin attacks him with lightning speed, leaping and kicking to try and gain a quick edge. No matter how they are set in a scene, chucks always manage to catch your eye.

Stills from Sin City.

Chucks as Part of the Story Line

A **FEW FILMS HAVE** even used the Chuck Taylor shoe as a plot point. In *The Cure* (1995), there are two emotional scenes where a black high-top serves as a symbol of the unlikely friendship that has developed between two eleven-year-old boys, Erik (Brad

Renfro), a disaffected loner from a dysfunctional family, and Dexter (Joseph Mazello), his next-door neighbor suffering from AIDS. In *Blood Work* (2002), the camera focuses on a bloody chuck footprint at a crime scene while Detective Ronaldo Arrango (Paul Rodriguez) tells FBI agent Terry McCaleb (Clint Eastwood), who is leading the investigation of a serial killer, "We know who our killer is. His name is Chuck . . . Chuck Taylor." As McCaleb is leaving the crime

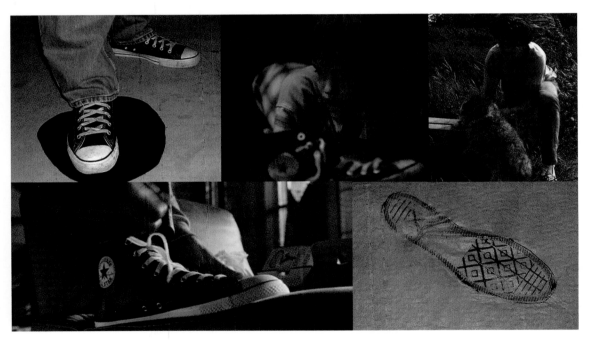

Clockwise from upper left: About to leave a tell-tale footprint; Dexter receiving a black high-top to hang on to; Danny uses his white high-top to signal danger to his family; a Chuck Taylor shoe leaves a very distinctive footprint; Del Spooner lacing up his vintage leather high-tops in the year 2035.

★

scene and walking through the lines of cops, reporters, and curious onlookers, he happens to spy someone in the back of the crowd wearing a pair of what appears to be bloody white chucks. And the chase is on! In *I, Robot* (2004), set in a futuristic Chicago in the year 2035, Del Spooner (Will Smith) is a homicide detective who has a love-hate relationship with modern technology but loves to wear his vintage black leather high-top chucks. At the beginning of the film, Spooner gets out a brand-new pair, admires their look and feel, and then happily laces them up. Some things never change, as we hear other characters remark, "Cool shoes," about his chucks in later scenes. In *One Night at McCool's* (2001), Matt Dillon is wearing black high-top chucks in a scene where he has broken into a house and found a dead body. But he incriminates himself when he unknowingly steps in a pool of blood and leaves a tell-tale footprint. In *Running on Empty* (1988), River Phoenix played Danny Pope, the musically talented son of a family living in the underground on the run from the FBI since the late sixties. All he can take when they have to leave a town quickly is his practice keyboard, the clothes on his back, and his high-top chucks. In one of the opening scenes, you see Danny take off one of his chucks and tell their dog to take it to his younger brother. FBI agents have been spotted nearby and that is one of their family's signals to drop everything and run.

Comedies with Chucks

ANIMAL **H**OUSE **(1978)** features the comedy genius of John Belushi in a satire about a renegade fraternity that takes on the establishment of Faber College. Who can forget John "Bluto" Blutarsky, dressed in a pirate outfit plus black low-cut chucks, taking on the local ROTC and police as he leaps off buildings to create

★

general pandemonium during the homecoming parade? *Bill & Ted's Excellent Adventure* (1989) poses the interesting question, "What if the survival of the world depended on the academic success of two teenaged valley guys from southern California?" While this may sound frightening, the film is actually a campy send-up of how historical figures might react to our modern society. Bill and Ted both wear Chuck Taylor high-tops, and their contemporary suburban style of dress makes a statement in the film. Bill wears natural white high-tops with red laces, along with baggy jeans, white T-shirts, and cutoff sweatshirts or loose sweaters. Ted wears black high-tops with blue laces, gray thermal socks with a large red stripe, black surfer shorts over white cutoff sweatpants, a white T-shirt, and a black vest.

In *Encino Man* (1992), two Los Angeles high school losers dig up a frozen caveman in their

backyard, and when he thaws out they figure he is their ticket to being part of the "in" crowd at school. But the caveman (Brendan Frasier) turns out to be wilder and crazier than they ever imagined in this satire about the Stone Age meeting Generation X. Decked out in his valley-dude outfit of loose T-shirt, open vest, plaid shorts, gray thermal socks with a red top stripe, and worn black chuck high-tops,

Wayne and Garth broadcasting from Wayne's basement (top left); Gib trying to impress Allison in The Sure Thing *(bottom left); Bill and Ted playing air guitar (right).*

★

caveman Link fits right into the local scene, and the camerawork picks this up all through the film. The best sequence is saved for the prom, where Link wears a new pair of black checkered high-tops with red laces as he leads the crowd of partygoers in a wild dance sequence. *Wayne's World* (1992) is the first of two feature films based on the popular *Saturday Night Live* comedy segment. Wayne Campbell (Mike Myers) and Garth Algar (Dana Carvey) are two young guys into the heavy metal scene who broadcast a weekly program on the Aurora, Illinois, public-access channel. Black high-top chucks are a basic part of their standard metal scene attire, which includes long hair, torn Levi's, and dark T-shirts.

In *The Sure Thing* (1985), Walter "Gib" Gibson (John Cusack) is a chucks-wearing freshman at an Ivy League school, hoping to impress girls and get some romance in his life. In his English class, he notices Allison (Daphne Zuniga) who is attractive, articulate, and totally disinterested in any of Gib's advances. But he is eventually able to get Allison to tutor him in English. When his best friend back home in California tells him that he has set up a "sure thing" for him over Christmas break, he arranges a ride back there with a married couple. Things get interesting when the other rider in the car turns out to be Allison. As he does in many of his films, Anton Yelchin plays the title role of wealthy and intelligent teenager in *Charlie Bartlett* (2007), wearing his favorite sneaker on and off the set—black high-top chucks. Chucks are the equalizer in Charlie's outfits, which consist of expensive, preppy clothes. Charlie's black high-top chucks are a symbol of his desire to be seen as different and cool instead of an aloof one percenter. After being expelled from a series of private schools, Charlie must attend a public high school where he at first has trouble fitting in and is harassed by school bully Murphy Bivens (Tyler Hilton). All Charlie really wants to do in life is reach out to society. As he begins to better understand the social structure at the school, Charlie enlists Bivens to help him become the resident underground counselor to other students, giving out advice and prescription drugs that he gets from his own sessions with psychiatrists. He also falls in love with the principal's daughter, tangles with the school district hierarchy, and learns to deal with his own family problems in this coming-of-age comedy.

Adventures with Chucks

THROUGH THE MAGIC of the camera, we see chucks in action all over the world. Danny Rich (Ice Cube) wears black high-top chucks to tackle the Amazon River wilderness and giant snakes in *Anaconda* (1997). In *The Black Stallion Returns* (1983), Alec (Kelly Reno) struggles to cross the Sahara Desert in his black high-top chucks to find the black stallion when it is forcibly taken back to northern Africa by the Berber tribe. When his mother dumps his pair of white high-top chucks on his chest and tells him to make something out of his life, Brian McNichols (Bernie Coulson) has some *Adventures in Spying* (1992) tracking down a notorious drug smuggler whom he discovers hiding out in their small Washington town. Young Xan (Alex Michaeletos) undertakes a trek across the treacherous Kalahari Desert, the rapids of the Oka-vango Delta, and the wildlife reserves of South Africa to return his pet cheetah *Duma* (2005) to its native habitat. The condition of Xan's optical white chucks is one of the ways to measure how taxing and difficult the journey becomes. When the journey starts they are a normal broken-in pair of white high-tops, but by its end the canvas has become completely brown and torn. Benny (Marc Riffon), a kid from the wrong side of the tracks, wears his black high-tops through the wilderness areas of the Cascade Mountains in *White Wolves: A Cry in the Wild II* (1993). Benny and the other teenaged members of his party must learn to work together when their guide and teacher falls off a cliff and they have to figure out how to rescue him. In *The Protector* (2006), Tony Jaa performs an incredible series of martial arts battles wearing black high-tops as he tries to retrieve two stolen elephants taken by a well-connected gang of smugglers from Thailand to Australia. Moritz Bleibteu plays Manni, a petty criminal who has only twenty minutes to turn over money to gangsters or face death, in the European cult film *Run Lola Run* (1998). Lola (Franka Potente) hurries to help Manni. We see Manni running around the streets of Berlin in a pair of well-worn black high-top chucks as the film plays out a series of possible endings to their dilemma.

★

Paul and Danny on the Amazon River (upper left); Alec struggles to cross the Sahara Desert (upper right); Xan in the wildlife preserves of South Africa (middle left); Benny and Pandra hiking in the Cascade Mountains (middle right); fight scene from The Protector (bottom left); Manni and Lola running away from the police (bottom right).

All Star Drama

OVER THE YEARS there have been some outstanding performances by young actors wearing black high-top chucks. In *The Client* (1994), a strong ensemble cast led by Susan Sarandon, Tommy Lee Jones, and Ossie Davis delivers effective performances in this well-made screen adaptation of the John Grisham novel about a young boy pursued by both the Mafia and the FBI when he witnesses the suicide of a mob lawyer. Brad Renfro (in his film debut) looks and plays the part superbly as the indigent kid with attitude—dressed in baggy camouflage pants, rock music T-shirts, a jacket with the sleeves whacked off, and black high-top chucks—angry and hostile to the outside world, yet trying to be protective and caring for his mother and traumatized younger brother. In *The Climb* (1997), twelve-year-old Danny Hines (Gregory Smith) is challenged to prove his courage in a coming-of-age story set in suburban Baltimore in the late fifties. He must climb a huge but decrepit radio tower with nothing but his wits, his black high-top chucks, and help from a cranky neighbor who is a retired civil engineer. In *Mr. Holland's Opus* (1995), a film about the thirty-year struggle of a music teacher in the public schools, there is a great sequence of scenes in which Mr. Holland (Richard Dreyfus), as a favor to the track coach, agrees to teach percussion to Louis Russ (Terrence Howard), one of the school's star athletes, so that he can stay eligible by playing in the band. At first

Attorney Reggie Love meets with her client Michael Sway.

★

131

Russ has real trouble keeping a beat, so much so that Holland finally grabs his black high-top by the laces and taps it on the floor for him until he gets the concept of steady pulse. *A History of Violence* (2005) reminds us never to push someone too far. There is an incredible scene where teenager Jack Stall (Ashton Holmes) has a run-in with Bobby, a high school jock who has been bullying him for a long time. While walking in the hall with his girl-friend, Jack is pushed from behind into another student by Bobby, who taunts him over the fact that his dad is supposed to be a hero, yet Jack is such a wimp. This time the restraint in Jack snaps, and with some eerie similarities to an earlier scene with his father and two thugs, Jack quickly takes out Bobby and his friend in such decisive and brutal fashion that Bobby is sent to the hospital and Jack is suspended from school. The footwork with Holmes's black high-top chucks is amazing in this scene.

Gregory Smith takes on a huge radio tower in The Climb (top).

Mr. Holland grabs Russ's black high-top to help him learn where the beat is (bottom).

Several poignant dramas feature chucks-wearing teens and preteens facing death from cancers. In *Ways to Live Forever*, twelve-year-old Sam (Robbie Kay), suffering from terminal leukemia, decides to create a video journal so that his memory can live on. Shailene Woodley plays Hazel, a teenager with weakened lungs who must live with an oxygen tank in *The Fault In Our Stars*. Her cynical attitude about her condition changes when she meets fellow cancer sufferer Gus (Ansel Elgort), whose infectious charm, optimism, and desire for romance turns her life around. In *Death of a Superhero* (2012), Thomas Brody-Sangster plays a dying fifteen-year-old boy who draws comic-book images of an invincible superhero on his white high-top chucks and elsewhere as he struggles with his mortality. Writer/director Richard Linklater has made several films that feature chucks, including *Dazed and Confused* (1993), about the culture of high school students in a small Texas town in 1976; *Boyhood* (2014), his Best Picture–nominated tour-de-force shot over twelve years where we watch young Mason (Ellar Coltrane) grow up from the age of six until he enters college; and *Before Sunrise* (1995), a love story about two strangers who meet on a train to Vienna, hit it off, and embark on a romantic adventure for one night, knowing that they may never see each other again. Other romantic films where the lead male character wears black high-top chucks are *Pie in the Sky* (1996), *Fire with Fire* (1986), and *Blind Dating* (2006), where Chris Pine plays Danny, a blind man who is struggling to find the right woman.

Top row, left to right: Sam worrying about his fate in Ways to Live Forever; *Hazel suffers from weakened lungs in* The Fault in Our Stars; *Amy and Josh have their first romantic moment in* Pie in the Sky; *Jesse and Celine exchange their thoughts in* Before Sunrise. *Bottom row, left to right: Danny talks to his analyst in* Blind Dating; *Mason and his dad about to go swimming in* Boyhood; *dance scene from* Fire with Fire; *Jack retaliates against the bully Bobby in* The History of Violence.

★

Chucks for the Whole Family

AS YOU MIGHT imagine, there is a lot of good chucks footage to be seen in family-oriented films. In *The Baby-Sitters Club* (1995), we are introduced to Kristy (Schuyler Fisk) while the camera focuses on her worn, unbleached white high-tops. These chucks are her favorite footwear, which she always wears with denim and backward caps. Besides the opening sequence, there are good closeups of her walking when she meets up with her dad, dances for the kids, and best of all when she receives the chuck lover's favorite birthday present—a brand-new pair of high-top chucks. Besides Kristy, her father, Patrick (Peter Horton), wears black high-tops in most of his scenes, and many of the summer camp kids wear black, blue or red high-tops. In *Heaven Sent* (1994), Eddie Chandler (Vincent Kartheiser) wears black high-top chucks throughout the film. They help define his look and image as a rebellious, at-risk kid, and they fit very well with his loose and baggy clothes look that you see among today's teenagers. The best chucks scene is during a confrontation with Howard, Eddie's guardian angel. When Eddie tries to go off in the wrong direction, he finds that his chucks are glued to the sidewalk until he agrees to do the right thing. In order for this scene to look right, and for Eddie's chucks to stay firmly connected to the ground while he tries to walk away in them, a pair of black high-tops had to be literally nailed into the cement.

Kristy meets her biological father who has suddenly come back into her life in The Babysitters Club.

★
134

Sky High (2005) stars Michael Angarano as Will Stronghold, the son of two superheroes and a freshman in a high school for the children of people with special powers. Will wears red high-top chucks throughout the film as he tries to find a balance between being a normal teenager and the expectations that he will be another superhero. His problem is that he doesn't know what his power is. With all of the stunts in the film and the chucks-friendly cinematography by Shelly Johnson, you often see closeups during the struggles between Stronghold and his opponents. But the best chucks scene has to be the sequence where he has just received his first kiss from his new girlfriend, Gwen. Will, exhilarated by the experience, flies through the air to the streetlight in front of her house, circles around the light, and then lands in the street when the light comes crashing down. In *Tommy Tricker and the Stamp Traveler* (1987), a Canadian family classic with a stamp-collecting theme, Ralph (Lucas Evans) and Tommy (Anthony Rogers) wear high-top chucks during most of the film, and chucks even appear on actual postage stamps when they go "stamp traveling." Director of photography Andreas Poulsson deserves credit for his approach to the cinematography of the film, which continually shows us chucks shots in almost every scene. With their rising popularity among young girls, you now see more instances of chucks being worn by lead girl actresses, like the black high-tops worn by Dakota Fanning in *Charlotte's Web* (2006),

Black high-top chucks nailed to the cement during the shooting of Heaven Sent.

and white knee-highs by AnnaSophia Robb in *The Bridge to Terabithia* (2007).

More recent family movies include the Diary of a Wimpy Kid series (2010–12) starring Zachary Gordon. We watch his character Greg struggle through adolescence with his family and friends and at school. The cine-

Will lands in the street after flying around a streetlight in front of Gwen's house in Sky High.

matography is very chucks friendly and Greg's black high-top chucks are prominently shown throughout all three movies. Through all of his troubles, missteps, and screw-ups, they are the one cool thing Greg has going for him. *Jinxed* (2013) is the story of a family cursed with bad luck and how their two kids work to remove it. Brett (Jack Griffo), Charlie (Jacob Bertrand), and Meg (Ciara Bravo) wear chucks in the film, with the most prominent wearer being Charlie, famous on YouTube for his wipeout skateboard videos. *The Boy Who Cried Werewolf* (2010), another Nickelodeon film, is about a single dad, who is trying to make ends meet, and his chucks-wearing son and daughter (Chase Ellison and Victoria Justice) who attempt to gain acceptance at their high school. Everything changes when the family inherits a castle in Tran-sylvania from a deceased uncle. Imagine kids in chucks trampling down dark corridors where vampires and werewolves live. In the third installment of Disney's High School Musical franchise, Troy (Zac Efron) wears black high-top chucks as he romances Gabriella (Vanessa Hudgens) through a series of well-staged and technically perfect dance sequences. Other recent films of note are *The Adventures of Mickey Matson and the Copperhead Conspiracy* (2013), *Smitty* (2012), and *Hotel for Dogs* (2009), which is about two orphaned foster kids (Emma Roberts and Jake T. Austin in red low-cuts) who are not permitted to keep their pet dog, and they secretly set up a shelter for stray dogs at a vacant hotel. In *Lassie* (1994), a feature film based on the classic television series, the lead character Matt (Tom Guiry) wears black or maroon high-top chucks throughout the film.

There are some interesting family films from Europe with young actors wearing chucks. *Blinker en de Blixvaten* (Blinker and the Blix Barrels, 2008) is a Flemish film about teenagers Blinker Van Steen (Kasper Vanbeginne, chocolate brown chucks) and his girlfriend, Nelle (Lynn Van de Velde, plaid print chucks), who both wear high-

Greg settling down for a day of kicking back and playing video games (upper left); Ralph goes stamp traveling (upper right); Hunter and Jordan at a cemetery with Madame Varcolac (bottom left); still of Brett, Charlie, Meg, and Ivy in Jinxed (bottom right).

tops. When his father is mistakenly arrested for toxic waste pollution, Blinker and Nelle take on the ruthless young executives and goons of Blix Industries who are the real culprits. In *The Fakir* (Fakiren fra Bilbao, 2004), teenaged twins Emma (Julie Zangenberg, red high-tops) and Tom (Alsel Leth, black high-tops) move into a large, ramshackle house in the Danish countryside along with their recently widowed mother, Louise. Although unhappy about their family situation, the twins have little time to worry about that when they discover that the house is haunted by a ghost hidden in a ballpoint pen and that it contains a hidden treasure actively sought by two determined bad guys. Great special-effects highlight *Island of Lost Souls* (2007), the

Zac Efron and Vanessa Hudgens star in the High School Musical series (top left); Young "Goose" and his new dog, Mutt, bond in Lost Christmas *(top right); Oskar and Josefine time travel to the sixteenth century (bottom left); Scipio, the Thief Lord, at a costume shop in Venice (bottom right).*

story of three kids and a disillusioned spirit hunter living in a small Danish town who fight against a malevolent supernatural force trying to take over the world. *Oskar & Josefine* (2005) is about two twelve-year-old kids from Copenhagen who visit Oskar's (Mikkel Konyher) grandparents for the summer. Josefine (Pernille Kaae Høier) receives a medallion from a man they meet that allows the two to time travel four hundred years into the past, where they interact with Oskar's ancestors.

There is a funny line about Oskar's chocolate high-top chucks when one of the elders from the seventeenth century takes a disparaging look at Oskar and Josefine in their contemporary garb of shorts, T-shirts, and sneakers and asks, "Is that the way people are dressing in Copenhagen these days?" A year after he was orphaned on Christmas day in *Lost Christmas* (2011), young Goose (Larry Mills, black high-tops) meets an enigmatic stranger with apparent psychic powers who begins to change his life. In *Den korsikanske biskopen* (The Corsican Bishop, 1993), Swedish cousins Kalle (Oliver Loftéen, black high-tops) and Max (David Fornander) follow the clues left by Kalle's late father to find a rain-making waterwheel. And in *The Thief Lord* (2006), Scipio (Rollo Weeks, navy high-tops) helps orphaned and other abandoned kids in Venice hide from the authorities while teaching them to support themselves through petty thievery.

★

Chucks Break a Leg

CHUCKS HAVE A role in two of America's most influential musicals. *West Side Story* was first performed on Broadway in 1959 and then made into a 1961 film that won numerous Academy Awards. Chucks are part of the trend-setting costuming, which has the Jets wearing white low-cuts, and the Sharks wearing black low-cuts, the first example of gangs identified by the color of their sneakers. *Grease* is the word and black high-top chucks are the footwear in the 1978 Hollywood remake of the popular Broadway musical. There are lots of chucks being worn in this film, one of the great things about the fifties, and you see them in the backgrounds of many of the scenes. Three of the T-Bird guys wear them, and, of course, so do all of the athletes and a lot of the students at Rydell High. It's nice to see a film where students train in them, dance in them, wear them to class, and just fool around in them. Probably the best scene for chucks is when Danny (John Travolta) decides to impress Sandy (Olivia Newton-John) by going out for sports at Rydell. You see the entire basketball team, wrestling team, and track team working out with black high-tops. Even the coach (Sid Caesar) sports a pair of white high-tops.

Grease is the word, and high-top chucks are the footwear from this popular musical.

★

Science Fiction and Fantasy Films with Chucks

THE **TYPICAL SCIENCE** fiction or fantasy film is often focused on the future, with an emphasis on robots and other creatures with a futuristic look or demons and mythological creatures. But chucks do occasionally appear. We have already mentioned Will Smith lacing up his leather high-top chucks in *iRobot*. In the 2014 release of *The Amazing Spider-Man 2*, Andrew Garfield wears black high-tops whenever he is acting as Peter Parker. There are a couple of great shots—one of Peter sitting on the pinnacle of a tall building in New York as he wears a pair, and another of an empty pair that he has just dashed out of to put on his Spider-Man costume.

Teo Halm in Earth to Echo *(top left), Emma Watson, Rupert Grint, and Daniel Radcliffe in* Harry Potter and the Half-Blood Prince *(top right), Andrew Garfield and Dane DeHaan in* The Amazing Spider-Man 2 *(bottom left), the flying black high-top chuck in* Percy Jackson & the Olympians: The Lightning Thief *(bottom right).*

★

Watching the Harry Potter film series, you were never quite sure what time frame you were in until the fifth film, *Harry Potter and the Order of the Phoenix* (2007). We see first see Harry (Daniel Radcliffe) sporting a pair of black low-cut chucks as he is being attacked by the Dementors, as well as throughout the film as he takes on the evil forces of Lord Voldemort. Harry also wears them in *Harry Potter and the Half Blood Prince* (2009). *Percy Jackson & the Olympians: The Lightning Thief* (2009) is a modern-day action-adventure film featuring characters from mythology. Percy (Logan Lerman) is on a quest to retrieve three pearls that will allow him and his fellow warriors to transport to the underworld, where they can retrieve a missing lightning bolt belonging to Zeus. He is having great difficulty until his friend Luke gives him a pair of winged black high-top chucks, a contemporary version of Hermes's winged sandals. Other recent films in this genre include *Push* (2009), *Robot Overlords* (2014), *Frequency* (2000), and *Eternal Sunshine of the Spotless Mind* (2004). *D.A.R.Y.L.* (1985) and *Starman* (1984) are classic science fiction films that feature chucks. At the end of *Starman*, you see the Starman (Jeff Bridges), walking into the energy field of the mother ship, taking his chucks with him into space. You wonder if the aliens will figure out why they don't slip or slide and what they think of the star logo on the side.

Chucks in Horror Films

CHUCKS ARE OFTEN seen in horror films, worn by teens and young twenty-something characters who are about to have something bad happen to them. In that sense they are a symbol of innocence. Most of the characters in the following films wear black high-top chucks. *The Haunting in Connecticut* (2009) is about the supernatural experiences of Matt (Kyle Gallner), a teenager suffering from cancer. When his family moves into an old country house close to where Matt goes for specialized radiation treatments, strange things begin to happen. Matt, and later his siblings, continually sees apparitions and hears the sounds of a haunted house possessed by the spirits of horrible crimes that had been committed there in

★

Belch is slowly sucked down a pipe by the force of the monster.

the past. With the help of a clergyman, Matt and the others work to exorcise the evil spirits and break free of their control. *Hellphone* (2007) is part teen romance, part comedy, part horror, part fantasy, and part coming-of-age beautifully shot in a single film. Its uniquely French outlook on American teen cultural norms is quite captivating and funny, with visual treats like scenes with young Sid (Jean-Baptiste Maunier) and his buddy Tiger (Benjamin Jungers) skateboarding the streets of Paris in pairs of mismatched high-top chucks. James Muth's script is a tongue-in-cheek commentary on the obsession with smartphones that has gripped the younger generation, finally manifested in the plotline when Sid's Hellphone takes over his life and begins committing all kinds of horrific acts. Other interesting films in the genre are *Brainscan* (1994), starring Edward Furlong as a teenager obsessed with horror films who gets the chance to play an interactive game about murder; *Ice Cream Man* (1995), in which almost all the characters wear chucks; *Jeepers Creepers* (2001), Victor Salva's stylish tale starring Justin Long who literally falls into a culvert filled with dead bodies; *Lady in White* (1988), which pits a young boy (Lukas Hass) against a serial killer when he sees an apparition re-enacting the murder of a young girl; *The Paperboy* (1994), which is about a murderous kid who wears red high-top chucks; *Saw II* (2005), where Daniel (Erik Knudsen) is locked up with a group of people in a booby-trapped house; and Rob Zombie's 2007 remake of John Carpenter's *Halloween*, where we see young Mike Myers (Daeg Faerch) and scared babysitter Laurie Strode (Scout Taylor-Compton) both wearing black high-top chucks. *It* (1990) is an adaptation of the Stephen King novel about a recurring malevolent predatory force terrorizing a New England town, and it has many characters wearing black high-top chucks, including

★

Ben (Brandon Crane), Bill (Jonathan Brandis), Richie (Seth Green), and Eddie (Adam Faraizl), along with Belch (Drum Garrett) and several of the other town bullies. Additionally, we see Mike (Marlon Taylor) wearing white low-cut chucks. There are lots of good shots throughout all of the scenes set in 1960, but you won't forget the scene where Belch is taken by the dead, white light of "It" as it stands him up in its force field and pulls him down a drainage pipe, the soles of his chucks the last thing you see before he disappears.

Chucks in Sports Films

NO **DISCUSSION** **ABOUT** the Chuck Taylor in films would be complete without mentioning the best sports films that have chucks in them. The number one film has to be *Hoosiers* (1987). This classic story of a small town basketball team that comes from nowhere to the Indiana state finals is considered by critics to be one of the best sports film ever made. This film is worth a look just to return to the days when teams were defined by their black or white Chuck Taylor high-tops. All of the basketball games contain great chucks shots, either black vs. black, or black vs. white. But as you peruse the entire movie, the best scene has to be in the regional finals, where one of the weakest players is brought in at the end of the game, is fouled,

Coach Dale takes over the Hickory High School basketball team.

and has to make the game winning shot. The camera pans up from his chucks into his face as he takes the team to the state finals. Great stuff that all young hoopsters' dreams are made of!

Other basketball films worthy of mention include *Glory Road* (2006), which is the story of how Texas Western coach Don Haskins led the first all-black starting line-up for a college basketball team to the NCAA national championship in 1966. In *One on One* (1977), young Henry Steele (Robby Benson), a high school basketball star from a small town, comes to Los Angeles to participate in big time college basketball. But Henry is quickly overwhelmed by the corruption of the system and the overbearing coach. Soon he finds himself fighting for his scholarship and college career. *The Pistol: The Birth of a Legend* (1991) is the story of how young Pete Maravich began to pursue his dream to become one of the world's greatest basketball players with the support and encouragement of his father, a visionary basketball coach at Clemson University. The film is set during Pete's early high

Young Pete Maravich works on his dribbling skills.

school years, when he was a freshman on the Daniel High School varsity team. Young Pete lives in black-and-optical white high-tops, so the film is filled with great chucks shots from beginning to end.

The Basketball Diaries (1995) is based on an autobiographical novel by Jim Carroll, who is played in the film by Leonardo DiCaprio. The film focuses on Jim and his friends, who are on a basketball team in a Catholic high school in New York City. From the start of the film, the boys demonstrate a totally hedonistic and immoral

Leonardo DiCaprio in The Basketball Diaries *(left),* Sylvester Stallone in Rocky.

attitude toward life. They are involved in hard drug use and as they become more addicted, they lose their athletic skills and gradually turn to violent criminal behavior to support their addictions. Carroll's one redeeming feature in the plot line is that he is an aspiring author, who keeps a diary of his life, even through the most destitute of times and experiences. There are great black high-top chucks shots throughout much of the film, as DiCaprio and his buddies on the team wear them most of the time. But the story line is progressively more depressing, and it makes you wonder how these kids could enter into such a depraved lifestyle so quickly.

Chucks also make appearances in films about other sports. *Rocky* (1976), Sylvester Stallone's first boxing film, stands up over time as one of the best sports films ever made. The training sequence where Rocky, wearing black high-top chucks, runs through town and up the steps of the Philadelphia Museum of Art to "Gonna Fly Now" is a classic film moment. *Breaking Away* (1979) is about a young champion cyclist living in a college town who wants to spend the year after high school just hanging around, competing in races, and having fun with his three best friends. But reality soon changes their lives in this Academy Award–winning coming-of-age film. Two good baseball films about kids are *Rookie of the*

★
145

Year (1993) and *The Sandlot* (1993). *Dodgeball: A True Underdog Story* (2004) takes on all the clichés of sports films and proceeds to give you a humorous twist on each. In *Across the Tracks* (1991), Rick Schroeder and Brad Pitt play two brothers, one recently released from reform school and the other a track star trying to qualify for a scholarship to Stanford University, who conflict with each other over lifestyles and eventually on the running track. Throughout the film, Rick Schroeder in his role as Billy wears black high-top chucks. He even wears them while running track, again reminding us that chucks are great shoes for many sports. Toward the end of the film, Brad Pitt also wears white high-tops in several of the scenes.

Television Shows with Actors Wearing Chucks

THE **CHUCKSCONNECTION HAS** documented over ten dozen television series where a main actor has worn chucks. With television, there is a lot less continuity in the dress of a character because costuming for a show often changes throughout the episodes and seasons of a series. Television shows tend to be shot in a smaller screen frame with more

Sara Moulton with pink high-tops (left); The Odd Squad *cast (right).*

close-ups and extreme close-ups than films, so you are less likely to see a character's footwear in a lot of the scenes.

Over the years, there have been hosts for cooking, home-improvement, and variety or activity shows who wear chucks. *About Your House* (PBS, 1996–2001), a home-repair and improvement show, was hosted by Bob Yapp, who wore chucks in different colors on the show. Ty Pennington, the design team leader and carpenter on *Extreme Makeover: Home Edition* (ABC, 2003–07), often wore low-cut chucks in blue and Carolina blue. On *Cooking Live* (FNT, 1997–2002), host Sara Moulton wore high-top chucks of various colors on her show. Ellen Degeneres often wears low-cut chucks in various colors on her NBC daily talk and variety show, and the logo of her production company is a pair of blue or black low-cut chucks. Linda Ellerbee is noted for wearing bright orange or red high-tops on her shows and specials. *Zoom* (PBS, 1999–2005) featured an ensemble cast of middle school–aged kids who demonstrated games, activities, and various projects on screen. All of the kids wore black low-cuts, a sort of unisex tribute to chucks. The *Odd Squad*, shown on TVOKids in Canada and PBS Kids in the United States since 2014, features a team of kids who wear formal attire and high-top chucks while they use reasoning and mathematics to investigate and solve strange happenings in their town.

The Wonder Years

WHEN YOU LOOK at television shows that feature actors wearing chucks, the powerhouse series has to be *The Wonder Years* (ABC). The show was about how adolescents, as seen through the eyes of Kevin Arnold (Fred Savage), dealt with the issues of growing up in the 1960s. Kevin's experiences

★

Kevin and his friends check out the sexuality manual in The Wonder Years.

are narrated by him as an adult (the voice of Daniel Stern), and describe his various relationships with other kids, his family, and adults. All the male characters usually have on chucks. Kevin is seen wearing both white and black high-tops, and his older brother Wayne wears black low-cuts and sometimes high-tops. Winnie, Kevin's on-again, off-again girlfriend, wears maroon low-cuts in the pilot episode. Even the physical education teacher wears black high-tops, and once in a while you see Kevin's dad wearing white low-cut chucks.

Classic Television Shows

DENNIS THE MENACE (CBS, 1959–63) was an adaptation for television of the comic strip drawn by Hank Ketcham, and it starred Jay North as Dennis and Gale Gordon as Mr. Wilson. Dennis was always seen in his outfit of overalls, striped T-shirt, and black Chuck Taylor high-tops. *Happy Days* (ABC, 1974–84) was developed to take advantage of the nostalgia craze for the fifties, which became popular in the 1970s. In the show, Richie Cunningham (Ron Howard) often wore white high-tops, and one of the later characters, Chachi

Allan Kayser, Ken Berry, Dorothy Lyman, and Vickie Lawrence in Mama's Family.

★

Chucks in the Media

★ ★

(Scott Baio), wore black high-tops. Most of the guys from Jefferson High School who hung out at Arnold's Drive-In, a malt shop near the high school, wore black chucks. *Laverne and Shirley* (ABC, 1976–83) was a spin-off from *Happy Days* about two girls who worked on the assembly line in a brewery. The writing was mostly slapstick, and it featured screwball characters like Lenny (Michael McKean) and Squiggy (David Lander), two truck drivers at the plant who often wore black high-tops. Shirley's boyfriend was Carmine Ragusa (Eddie Mekka) who wore black low-cuts. The classic "boy and his dog" series *Lassie* (CBS, 1954–71) went through many changes during its seventeen-year run. The one feature that remained the same was, of course, Lassie (although she was portrayed by many different collies over the years). For the first three years of the series, it was called *Jeff's Collie* and the stories revolved around the Miller family, young Jeff (Tommy Rettig), his widowed mom, Ellen (Jan Clayton), and

Chachi and the Fonz in Happy Days.

his grandfather (George Cleveland). Jeff and his best friend Porky (Donald Keeler) were always seen wearing black high-top sneakers, and Jeff's were Chuck Taylors. In a much later Canadian version of *Lassie* (Animal Planet Network 1997–99), Cory Sevier wore red high-top chucks in the second season. *Mama's Family* (NBC, 1983–90) was a spin-off from one of the classic sketches on the Carol Burnett variety show about a humorously dysfunctional extended family living in Raytown, Missouri. In the third year of the show, a new character was added, teenager Bubba Higgins (Allan Kayser). Bubba ended up at the Harper household because his parents had left for Florida without telling him while he

★

was in juvenile hall for joyriding. Bubba was always chasing after the latest impractical craze or doing things that upset his grandmother, Thelma Harper (Vickie Lawrence). No matter the occasion, Bubba always wore maroon Chuck Taylor high-tops throughout the run of the series.

Jackass

JOHNNY KNOXVILLE STARRED in this MTV show (2000–02) about all kinds of crazy and sometimes controversial variations on stunts, dares, and situational antics, which were videotaped and then edited into short sequences on each show. Some of the stunts involve Knoxville himself, who is always wearing black high-top chucks on the show and in real life. This series was later made into four feature films. As a promotional tie-in to the second film, Converse issued a special line of "Jackass" chucks in 2006.

Johnny Knoxville.

BBC Shows

THE LONG-RUNNING SERIES, *Lovejoy* (1986–94), featured an antiques dealer and collector who often became embroiled in mysteries or scams involving the buying or selling of antiques. Sometimes on the edge of being unscrupulous, Lovejoy basically had a good heart and often used his sleuthing skills and knowledge of antiques to help someone out who had been swindled or who was in trouble. Lovejoy often wore black high-top chucks in the series. *Doctor Who* is a long-running British science fiction television series about a mysterious time-traveling adventurer known only as "the Doctor" who explores time and space with his companions, while fighting evil. The tenth Doctor Who (David Tennant) always wore a pair of high-top chucks (in various colors), along with his very English-looking three-piece suits, during his five years (2005–10) with the series. A spin-off show from the *Doctor Who* series, *The Sarah Jane Adventures* (2007–11), featured Elisabeth Sladen as a freelance journalist whose real occupation is saving the world from alien invaders. Sarah Jane was ably assisted by her neighbors, teenagers Clyde, Maria, and Rani, along with her adopted son, Luke. Luke was created by aliens in human form, and he turns out to be a boy wonder and genius who often helps save the day. In the third season, Luke starts to get hip and begins wearing black high-top chucks, as does his best friend, Clyde, who wears white high-tops.

Dramatic Series

SCORPION (ON **CBS** SINCE **2014**) is an American drama television series loosely based on the life of genius and computer expert Walter O'Brien, who recruits a team of other geniuses to help him solve complex, global problems. One of his team members is Toby Curtis (Eddie Kaye Thomas), who wears black high-top chucks in most of his scenes. In *Perception* (TNT 2012–15), Dr. Daniel Pierce (Eric McCormack) is an eccentric neuroscientist who uses his unique outlook on the mind and human behavior to help FBI agent Kate Moretti (Rachael Leigh Cook), a former student, solve complex criminal cases. Pierce is a popular professor at Lake Michigan University in Chicago. However, he suffers from bouts of schizophrenia on occasion, causing issues when he hears voices and sees imaginary people. Sometimes the hallucinations he sees help him solve the current case.

★

Cast of The Sarah Jane Adventures *(upper left); David Tennant and Billi Piper in* Doctor Who *(upper right); Eric McCormack as Dr. Daniel Pierce in* Perception *(lower left); Noah Crawford in* My Name Is Earl *(middle inset); Keri Russell is Felicity in* Felicity *(lower center); Eddie Kaye Thomas in* Scorpion *(lower right).*

Kate and Pierce's live-in teaching assistant, Max Lewicki (Arjay Smith), work to keep Dr. Pierce rooted in reality. He wears black or navy blue high-top chucks in the series. *Numb8rs* (CBS, 2005–10), another crime-drama series featuring a collaboration between a college professor and the FBI to solve crimes, revolved around the Eppes family. Don Eppes (Rob Morrow) leads a team of FBI agents. His younger brother, Charlie (David Krumholtz), is a brilliant mathematician at CalSci University who provides insight into current cases using his advanced knowledge of logic and numbers. The Epps family is rounded out by their widowed father, Alan (Judd Hirsch), who provides emotional support for his two very intense sons. In the second season, Charlie becomes romantically involved with Amita Ramanujan (Navi Rawat), another mathematician who often wears low-cut chucks.

In *Felicity*, new college freshman Felicity (Keri Russell) is all set to attend Stanford University with the full support of her parents, but suddenly, at her high school graduation, she realizes that she had missed out on a lot of life and is determined not to let that happen in college. On a whim, she applies to a New York City university where Ben (Scott Speedman), a boy she barely knew in high school but secretly admired, is attending. When she is accepted, her parents are devastated and cut off her financial support. But Felicity refuses to back down, and she goes to New York. The show is about her relationships with Ben and the other students she meets, and her drive to be independent. Felicity is seen wearing black low-cut chucks in many scenes in the series, which aired from 1998 to 2002 on the WB Television Network. In *Northern Exposure* (CBS, 1990–95), a series about life in a small Alaskan town, Ed Chigliak (Darren Burrows), a young Native American who has dreams of becoming a filmmaker, wears black Converse high-tops most of the time, weather permitting. *The O.C.* (Fox, 2003–07) was a fashion conscious prime-time soap opera that focused on a group of teenagers living in Newport Beach, a wealthy enclave in Orange County, California. Seth (Adam Brody) wore black high-top chucks in many of the episodes. *Psych* (USA, 2006–14) stars James Roday as young police

★

consultant Shawn Spencer who solves crimes with powers of observation so acute the precinct detectives think he's psychic—at least that's what he lets them believe. James Roday wears blue high-top chucks occasionally in the series and Young Shawn, played by Liam James, wears black high-tops in sixty flashback scenes. Similarly, young Earl (Noah Crawford) in *My Name Is Earl* (NBC, 2005–09) also wears black high-tops in flashback scenes.

Comedy and Family Series

THE BIGGEST COMEDY series hit on television in recent years is *The Big Bang Theory* (CBS, 2007–present). Roommates Leonard (Johnny Galecki) and Sheldon (Jim Parsons) have brilliant minds when it comes to science and physics, but they have trouble interacting with people, especially women. Sheldon is quite content to live life by his own quirky set of rules and spend time playing games with Howard Wolowitz (Simon Helberg) and Rajesh Koothrappali (Kunal Nayyar), two other socially dysfunctional CalTech scientists. All this begins to change when free-spirited Penny (Kaley Cuoco) moves in across the hall, and the guys start seeing the potential for love with her, and later Leslie (Sara Gilbert), Amy (Mayim Bialik), and Bernadette (Melissa Rauch). Leonard wears black low-cut chucks throughout the series. Another long-running comedy series is *The Middle* (ABC, 2009–present) about the Hecks, a somewhat oddball family living in Orson, Indiana. Perhaps the most "normal" family member is Axl (Charlie McDermott), conceived while his parents were listening to Guns N' Roses. Axl is a typical teenager, outgoing to others, lazy at home, and alternately fighting and supporting his family. Axl wears black high-top or low-cut chucks most of the time. *About a Boy* (NBC, 2014–15) focuses on the quirky relationship that develops between Will Freeman (David Walton), a single man who lives off the royalties of a hit song he wrote, and Marcus (Benjamin Stockham), an oddly charming but emotionally needy eleven-year-old who moves in next door and begins disrupting Will's perfect life. Marcus wears both red and black high-top chucks in different episodes. *Little People, Big World* (2006–14 on The Learning Channel) is a reality series about the Roloffs, an extraordinary family composed of both little and average-sized people. Parents Matt and Amy Roloff are both little people—four feet tall—but they are determined to succeed in a world that isn't always accepting of differences. Together they own and operate Roloff Farms, a sprawling thirty-four-acre farm in Oregon, where they raise four children: fifteen-year-old twins Jeremy and Zach, twelve-year-old Molly, and eight-year-old Jacob. Jeremy likes to wear Celtic green, red, and black and red foldover high-top chucks. For younger audiences, Nickelodeon

Top row, left to right: Stills from The Haunted Hathaways; The Big Bang Theory; and Spooksville. *Middle row:* Little People, Big World; Power Rangers Super Mega Force. *Bottom Row:* About a Boy; The Thundermans.

has several interesting series with lead characters wearing chucks. *The Haunted Hathaways* (2013–present) is about a family living in New Orleans who discovers there are three ghosts in their house. Taylor Hathaway (Amber Montana) often wears black high-top chucks, and Louie, one of the ghosts, is seen in a ghostly pair of grey high-top chucks. *The Thundermans*

★

(2013–present) is about a family of superheroes trying to maintain a normal life while leaning to deal with their superpowers. Young Billy (Diego Velasquez) speeds around in black or blue high-top chucks, and his older teen brother Max (Jack Griffo) occasionally wears black low-cuts. *Power Rangers Super Mega Force* is the twenty-first season of the Power Ranger franchise. The leader of the force is Tony Burrows (Andrew Grey), who wears black high-top chucks when he is not suited up in his Red Ranger garb.

Science Fiction/Fantasy on Television

ZACHARY LEVI IS Chuck in *Chuck* (NBC, 2007–12), head of the Nerd Herd geek squad at the local Buy More store. His life changes when he receives an email from a college friend that imbues his brain with the entire contents of an NSA/CIA computer filled with classified intelligence. The rival agencies both go after Chuck when they discover he has the information, but eventually he realizes that it gives him power over them. He ends up becoming part of their spy team, assisted by the stoic Colonel John Casey (Adam Baldwin) and the CIA's top agent, Sarah Walker. Chuck wears (what else!) black high-top chucks. *Continuum* (Showcase and Syfy, 2012–15) stars Rachel Nichols as a cop, Kiera Cameron, who is accidentally sent to 2012 from the year 2077 along with a terrorist group that the present day police and crime fighters are just not equipped to handle. Erik Knudsen plays Alec Sadler, a computer whiz who assists Kiera. Alec wears black low-cut chucks in every episode. *The Tomorrow People* (CW, 2013–present) are humans who have developed special powers (telepathy, teleportation, and telekinesis) as a result of genetic evolution. They are pursued by the Ultra, a paramilitary group of scientists, who are trying to control them. The series focuses on Stephen Jameson (Robbie Amell), who is just discovering his powers.

★

Stephen wears black high-top chucks with blue shoelaces in the series. *The Flash* (CW, 2014–present) is based on the DC Comic and is a spin-off from *The Arrow*, another popular series based on a comic book. Barry Allen (Grant Gustin) has the superpower of being able to move at lightning speed, something he obtained from an accident at a research lab after spending nine

The cast of Chuck *(top left); Eric Knudsen in* Continuum *(top right); Robbie Amell in* The Tomorrow People; *Hayden Panettierre in* Heroes *(bottom middle); fire burns a hole in the sole of Barry Allen's right sneaker in* The Flash *(bottom right).*

months in a coma. The series revolves around Barry's desire to clear his father's name—who was wrongly convicted of murdering his mother—and his work as a crime scene investigator. Grant Gustin wears black high-tops and other models of chucks in many of the episodes.

Heroes (NBC, 2006–10) was an epic drama that chronicled the lives of ordinary people who discover they possess extraordinary abilities. One of the main characters is high school cheerleader Claire (Hayden Panettiere). Both Claire and her boyfriend, Zach (Thomas Dekker), wear chucks in some of the episodes. *The Odyssey* (CBC, 1992–94) is a combination adventure and science fiction–fantasy series about Jay Ziegler (Illya Woloshyn), an eleven-year-old kid living in British Columbia. In the opening episode, Jay has a serious accident while playing and goes into

★

a coma, which is portrayed in the series as the Downworld, a surrealistic society run by warring factions of kids. Jay wears black high-top chucks throughout the first two seasons as he tries to find his way back home from the Downworld. *Roswell* (WB and UPN, 1999–2002) is about four teenagers who live among the citizens of Roswell, New Mexico, but who are actually human/ alien hybrids, sent here as replacements for the royalty of a dying alien race on the spaceship that crashed there in 1947. These hybrid aliens have special gifts, including the ability to heal fatal wounds. The crash had been covered up by the government, and these children were kept in incubation pods for ten years until they emerged as six-year-olds and were adopted by local families. Jason Behr plays Max Evans, one of the four aliens, and is often seen wearing black high-top chucks. The series mostly focuses on the various relationships that develop between the four kids and their human friends at Roswell High School. *Spooksville* (Hub, 2013–14) is based on the book series by acclaimed author Christopher Pike. Adam Freeman (Keann Johnson), the new kid in town, discovers that he holds the key to a battle between good and evil that has been taking place for centuries in Spooksville, a bizarre small town that plays host to a wide array of supernatural and unexplained occurrences. He is helped by two local teenagers, Watch (Nick Purcha), a genius who wears four wristwatches, and Sally Wilcox (Katie Douglas), who has knowledge of all the Spooksville legends and a crush on Adam. Watch wears natural white high-top chucks while Adam wears black low-cut chucks in many episodes.

Made-for-Television Films

THE **HALLMARK HALL** of Fame (on network television from 1951–2011, now on the Hallmark Channel) has been dedicated to bringing quality family programming in the form of feature-length special presentations for over sixty years. Programs on the series often dealt with family or social issues. Characters in these programs and even in their commercials were often seen wearing chucks. In *Journey* (1996), Jason Robards and Max

Max Pomeranc stars in Journey.

Pomeranc (Journey) are outstanding in this story of a restless mom who deserts her children and leaves them to be raised by their grandparents on the family farm. Through his love of photography, the grandfather helps Journey recover from the confusion and emptiness that he is experiencing and discover the true meaning of what a family is. *To Dance with the White Dog* (1993) starred Hume Cronyn and Jessica Tandy in one of their best collaborations. After fifty years of marriage, Sam Peek loses his beloved wife, Cora, and no amount of fussing by his overprotective children is going to ease Sam's loneliness or failing health, until a beautiful white dog appears out of nowhere one day and brings positive change to his life. The only problem—no one else can see this dog except his chucks-wearing grandson, Bobby (Harley Cross). *The Runaway*, which was broadcast in December 2000, deals with two young boys who are growing up in the post–World War II South, Luke and Sonny, one white and one black. They stumble on a murder mystery, and fears and prejudices are rekindled in their small town when they pretend to run away from home. Luke wears black high-top chucks throughout. Della Reese and Mason Gamble star in *Anya's Bell* (1999), which is about a blind woman who collects bells and never leaves her house. She suddenly finds herself alone when her mother dies. Anya meets Scott, another loner, a twelve-year-old boy from a single-parent family whom others term as slow, and they become friends. Together they help each other conquer personal handicaps. Scott aids the older woman in learning to use a walking cane so she can become mobile and better take care of herself, while Anya discovers that Scott's learning disability is due to dyslexia and not mental incapacity.

★

Chucks Are the "Sole" of Rock 'n' Roll

MANY ROCK MUSICIANS wear chucks. From AJR to the Zom-Zoms, there are lit-erally hundreds of popular bands worldwide that have at least one member who wears a pair of chucks on a regular basis. Why do so many musicians like chucks? James Sullivan, the pop music critic for the *San Francisco Chronicle*, described it this way: "For rock 'n' roll [bands], the shoe has an endlessly renewing legion of devotees. The members of the Strokes, rock 'n' roll's latest it-band, wear chucks. Classic punk bands like the Dead Boys and the Voidoids wore them. Hair bands of the 1980s such as Loverboy and Quiet Riot were partial to black chucks, while the Mighty Mighty Bosstones like the specialty plaid model." Part of the allure of chucks for many people is that when they see their favorite artists wearing the shoes, they want to emulate them by wearing chucks also.

The photo collage to the right shows musicians in all types of bands and solo artists who love wearing chucks. Chuck Taylor & the Dixie Squid is a Dixieland band who work out of Toledo, Ohio. Each band member wears a different colored pair of high-tops when they perform. This collage also features Winona Ryder wearing black low-cut chucks, James Hetfield of Metallica wearing black high-tops, and the Dingees, a Los Angeles–based band. The members of the band Ataris wear black low-cut chucks and all members of the punk rock band The Hunting-tons wear black high-top chucks, as do members of the bands The All-American Rejects and Stun. Jakob Dylan and the Wallflowers wear black high-top chucks or black Jack Purcells. David Johns from the band Silverchair wears navy blue high-tops. But even your local garage band is worthy of note if one or more members wear chucks. And if you think all these bands

are just made up of guys, check out the all-girl Swedish band Sahara Hotnights. Members of Green Day wear chucks, and so does one of the violinists from the Kronos String Quartet. Bruno Mars, Ed Sheeran, Robert Plant, Jason Mraz, and Wiz Khalifa are a few of the many solo artists who like wearing chucks.

With the development of the music video as an important way of presenting and marketing new songs, we see the presence of chucks in many of the videos. "You're Only Human (Second Wind)" was an early video from Billy Joel's DVD *The Essential Video Collection*

Stills from "One Foot" by fun. (clockwise from top left); "So Far Away" by Avenged Sevenfold; "Your Only Human (Second Wind)" by Billy Joel; and "Converse Girl" by the Buttons.

(2001, Columbia). The track is about George Young, a teenager living in the New York area who contemplates committing suicide after he wrecks his car and breaks up with his girlfriend. Joel plays a harmonica-playing friendly spirit who meets up with George as he is about to jump off a bridge. "Gangnam Style" by Psy (2012, YG Entertainment) took the world by storm in August 2012, and it not only climbed the charts but also was the first video on YouTube to have over one billion views. "Converse Girl" by The Buttons (2013, The Buttons Music) features not only snappy lyrics about chucks, but a video in which everyone is wearing them! It's pretty safe to say that the title of the song is its essence. "One Foot" (2012, Fueled by Ramen) by fun. is a lyric video where chucks are the star, and rightly so, as they have some of the lyrics written on them. Nothing hits home quite like a song about nostalgia, looking back, and cherishing those who made you what you are today. This rings true with Avenged Sevenfold's "So Far Away" (2010). Moving back and forth between flashbacks and the present, this tribute to their late drummer, Jimmy Sullivan, features a series of scenes from the band's past, showing more carefree versions of themselves growing up in their black high-top chucks.

Chucks in the Media

★ ★

Before concluding our examination of chucks in the media, let's take a look at a song about a pair of black high-top chucks. In 2003, songwriter and bluegrass artist Tim O'Brien released an album entitled *Traveler* on Sugar Hill Records.

The opening track on the album is called "Kelly Jose's Shoes." The lyrics of the song describe how a friend of his in Portland ended up giving him a pair of high-top chucks because they didn't fit him and "it looks like you've got travelin' to do."

Album cover for Traveler *by Tim O'Brien.*

The song goes on to portray some of his life on the road and what it is like for a musician to wear chucks:

Now I had a lot of fun in those black Chuck Taylors
A finer shoe has never been worn
I can see where I've been in the color fadin'
I can what I learned where they're frayed and worn

The song finishes by saying why he will continue wearing his chucks, in the spirit of so many other chucks fans:

These are shoes that like to travel,
No tellin' where they'll take me to
They're still not done scratchin' gravel
They still gotta show me a thing or two

chapter six

The Future of Chucks

DAVID MADDOCKS, CHIEF marketing officer for Converse in 2004, said, "We have a phrase we live by, which is, 'From our history we create our future.'" If you use that phrase as a guideline for the future of the Chuck Taylor sneaker, expect to see more cycles of great interest and then less interest in the fashion world, new generations discovering chucks for the first time, and the continued popularity of the basic core models. Fans of chucks who are interested in the entire line of models will continue to buy from Internet sites and from shoe and sporting goods stores in malls, while department stores will continue to carry limited lines of core and seasonal mod-

Chucks continue to be popular footwear for young people.

els for the general customer. Some people will buy them for fashion, some will buy them for comfort, and others will buy them for their active lifestyles and for their kids.

It's safe to say that the success of the Converse company is strongly tied to the success of the Chuck Taylor line of athletic shoes. Although the management remains top-down and secretive about their future plans, their overall direction is clear from their actions. In many ways, their plan emulates what Apple has done to become so successful in the last decade. Apple always maintained control over their line of products, never allowing anyone else to clone their operating systems while creating products that are seen as cool and hip by the public through clever product design, placement, celebrity endorsements, and ties with the entertainment community. They never compromised on the look or quality of their products

★

Interior of the San Francisco store.

Product display at the San Francisco store.

and kept their pricing on the high side. They vigorously fought against anyone who they felt violated their patents. Over the years Apple developed a dedicated set of consumers that continues to grow and will stand in lines to purchase their newest products.

Converse has been doing the same thing with their footwear products. Like Apple, they are fortunate to have very loyal and dedicated fans, especially for the Chuck Taylor line. Although there are still those who wish the manufacture would return to the United States, most fans have accepted the new order of things. Converse has helped in this transition by working diligently on quality control. There is a miniscule failure rate for their shoe products and the new chucks are very clean looking in their manufacture. In October of 2014, they filed lawsuits against thirty-one companies, including Walmart, Kmart, and Skechers, accusing them of trademark infringement by co-opting the look of their Chuck Taylor sneakers. Additionally, Converse filed a complaint with the International Trade Commission to block the import of wannabe chucks, calling them counterfeit. While some saw this move as mainly a public-relations play, there have already been some out-of-court settlements, and any legal action in the courts will likely play out over many years. As of this writing, Walmart and New Balance, who wasn't named in the original complaint but owns the PF Flyers brand, have vowed to fight Converse in court.

With chucks now retailing at a higher-than-average price for athletic shoes, Converse must work hard to keep their products in the public eye as cool fashion and not just another line of sneakers. There are three main facets to this: 1) continuing to produce clever and interesting variations on their Chuck Taylor, Jack Purcell, and Converse Con lines, 2) promoting their "design your own" program which encourages customers to create their own custom pairs, and 3) focusing on the relationship between Converse and the entertainment industry. This latter trend started with the issuance of rock-and-roll tribute chucks and now continues in their advertising, event sponsorships, and even facilities. In May of 2015, Converse opened a new world headquarters in Boston, where they will have larger presence in the public eye. The new facility includes its second Converse Rubber Tracks, a state-of-the-art music studio dedicated to providing emerging artists with the opportunity to record. CEO Jim Calhoun described it this way: "The opening of our new world headquarters is a momentous occasion for Converse. It brings us closer to the city's creative community, provides greater access to top talent, and we're thrilled to be here ushering in this new era for the brand."

Additionally, Converse is emulating the sales model set down by their parent company, Nike. Just like Nike, they have an active web business accompanied with a lot of online advertising, a national network of outlet stores, and, in some larger cities, large full-service retail stores like the Niketown stores. These flagship stores have over 8,000 square feet of sales area and offer the complete line of Converse footwear, clothing, and accessories. The stores have artistic designs such as the collage of hanging sneakers you see in the San Francisco store, as well as a room for in-store music performances and events. You can order your own custom-designed pair of Converse sneakers right at these store instead of online. And each store carries its own shoe, a city-themed print high-top Chuck Taylor.

In 1917, the Converse All Star will be one hundred years old, and in 2032, the Chuck Taylor All Star with his signed ankle patch will reach one hundred. Today, the core black-and-white high-top model has been in continuous manufacture since 1948, and the low-cut model since 1957. These are quite remarkable achievements for a simple canvas-and-rubber shoe, and no other athletic shoe has had an impact on our society like the Converse Chuck Taylor All Star.

The Future of Chucks

★ ★

Chucks were there for your parents, grandparents, and great-grandparents, and from all signs they will still be on the feet of your children, grandchildren, and great-grandchildren. Chucks have been a part of our lifestyle for so many years now that unless our way of living radically changes somehow, people will continue to lace them up as long as they are manufactured. Just remember what one of their early advertising jingles advised: "When your feet start to slip and slide, buy the sneaker with the star on the side." Con-VERSE! Limousines for the feet!

Acknowledgments
and Credits

Photos, illustration, and collages courtesy of **The ChucksConnection** or Classic Sports Shoes except as noted. Product advertisements from Converse are credited throughout the book. Information and quotes are from articles and features on **The ChucksConnection** website except as noted.

Introduction

"Chucks" definition from Jonathan Green. *The Dictionary of Contemporary Slang.* New York: Stein and Day, 1984.

Advertisement from the Converse Basketball Year Book, 1936, courtesy of the Joyce Collection, Notre Dame University.

Chapter 1

Tom DeLonge photo courtesy of www.blink182.com.

Fashion ad and Levis ad from *San Jose Mercury News* newspaper supplements.

Tre Cool photo courtesy of www.greenday.com.

Josh Moody, "'Chuck' Taylors," **The ChucksConnection**.

Doug Plocki quote from David Andrews, "Chucks Make Simple, Classic Fashion Sense," Penn State University *Collegian,* 1995.

Brett Staggs quote from Regis Behe, "Timeless Converse All Star Shoes Never Seem To Go Out of Style," *Pittsburgh Tribune-Review,* February 22, 2003.

Sam Cordova quote from Teresa Gubbins, "Fans of 'Chuck' Taylors Love Their Sneakers," *Dallas Morning News,* 2001.

★ ★

Bill Stearman quote from Britt Kennerly, "Chucks Go from Function to Fashion," *The Republic* (Columbus, IN), republic.com.

Beth Jones, "Guys Who Wear Chucks," *The Roanoke Times*, (Roanoke, VA).

Rick Majerus quote from Jack Wilkinson, "Converse All Stars Remain an Athletics Icon," *Atlanta Journal-Constitution*, 2001.

Cover illustration from the Converse Basketball Yearbook, 1961, courtesy of the Joyce Collection, Notre Dame University.

Chapter 2

For a complete biography of Chuck Taylor, refer to Abraham Aamidor's *'Chuck' Taylor, All Star*. Indiana University Press, 2006.

Quotes about Chuck Taylor's attendance at basketball games and his work selecting the All-America basketball team are from the Hall of Fame election article in the 1970 Converse Basketball Yearbook, page 50.

Quotes about 1990s advertising campaigns are from Kevin Goldman, "Converse Sneaker Bypasses Basketball Stars," *Wall Street Journal*, May 6, 1993.

Rick Burton quote from "The Cult of Converse," *Omaha World-Herald*, 2001.

Jack Boys quotes from Andy Murray, "Converse's Big Test," *New Hampshire Eagle-Tribune*, June 17, 2001.

Converse Yearbook pages thanks to the assistance of George Rugg, curator, Joyce Sports Collection, Hesburgh Library, Notre Dame University.

Core advertisement from Converse catalog.

Triumph band photo courtesy www.triumphmusic.com.

★

Chapter 3

Quotes about low-cut chucks are from the 1957 Yearbook ad shown in Chapter 2.
"Design your own chucks" shoe images were created using the converse.com interactive feature.
Gib Ford quote from Jack Wilkinson, "Converse All Stars Remain an Athletics Icon,"
    Atlanta Journal-Constitution, 2001.

Chapter 4

American Athletics staff and product photos courtesy of www.americanathletics.com.
Thanks to Corky Fulton and Gary Church for their time and hospitality as well as the information and quotes for this chapter.

Chapter 5

For more information about the films and television series described in this chapter, go to the Internet Movie Database, www.imdb.com, or see the listings and reviews on **The ChucksConnection**, chucksconnection.com.
Thrashin' still courtesy of MGM Home Entertainment.
The Skateboard Kid still courtesy of New Concorde Family Entertainment.
Back to the Future still courtesy of Universal Studios.
Sin City stills courtesy of Buena Vista Home Entertainment.
The Cure still courtesy of Universal Studios.

★

I, Robot still courtesy of Twentieth Century Fox Home Entertainment.
Running on Empty still courtesy of Warner Brothers Home Video.
Wayne's World still courtesy of Paramount Home Video.
Bill & Ted's Excellent Adventure photo courtesy of MGM Home Entertainment.
Anaconda still courtesy of Columbia TriStar Home Video.
Black Stallion Returns still courtesy of MGM Home Video.
Duma still courtesy of Warner Brothers Home Entertainment.
White Wolves: A Cry in the Wild II still courtesy of New Horizons Home Video.
The Protector still courtesy of Shahmongkolfilm Inteternation.
Run Lola Run still courtesy of Sony Picture Classics.
The Client still courtesy of Warner Brothers.
The Climb still courtesy of Spellbound Pictures.
Mr. Holland's Opus still courtesy of Buena Vista Home Entertainment.
Ways To Live Forever still courtesy of Kino Lorber, World Wide Motion Pictures.
The Fault in Our Stars still courtesy of Fox 2000 Pictures.
Pie in the Sky still courtesy of Image Entertainment.
Before Sunrise still courtesy of Warner Brothers.
Blind Dating still courtesy of 20th Century Fox.
Boyhood still courtesy of Universal Pictures.
Fire with Fire still courtesy of Paramount Pictures.
A History of Violence still courtesy of New Line Home Entertainment.
The Babysitters Club still courtesy of Columbia Pictures.
Heaven Sent production photo courtesy of Navarre Corporation.
Sky High still courtesy of Walt Disney Home Entertainment.
Diary of a Wimpy Kid still courtesy of 20th Century Fox.
Tommy Tricker and the Stamp Traveller still courtesy of Family Home Entertainment.

★

The Boy Who Cried Werewolf still courtesy of Nickelodeon.
Jinxed photo courtesy of Nickelodeon.
High School Musical 3 still courtesy of Walt Disney Home Entertainment.
Lost Christmas still courtesy of Impact Pictures.
Oskar & Josefine still courtesy of Cosmo Film.
The Thief Lord still courtesy of 20th Century Fox.
Grease still courtesy of Paramount Home Video.
Earth to Echo photo courtesy of 20th Century Fox.
Harry Potter and the Half Blood Prince still courtesy of Warner Brothers.
The Amazing Spider-Man 2 photo courtesy of Columbia Pictures.
Percy Jackson and the Lightning Thief still courtesy of Fox 2000 Pictures.
It still courtesy of Warner Brothers Home Video.
Hoosiers still courtesy of Hemdale Corporation.
The Pistol still courtesy of VCI Entertainment, www.vcient.com.
The Basketball Diaries still courtesy of Lions Gate Films.
Rocky still courtesy of MGM Home Video.
Sara Moulton photo courtesy of The Food Network.
The Odd Squad photo courtesy of PBS.
The Wonder Years still courtesy of the Black/Marlens Company.
Happy Days still courtesy of ABC.
Mama's Family still courtesy of Joe Hamilton Productions.
Johnny Knoxville photo courtesy of People's Choice Awards.
Sarah Jane Adventures still courtesy of BBC.
Perception still courtesy of TNT.
Doctor Who photo courtesy of BBC.
Felicity photo courtesy of Warner Brothers.
My Name Is Earl still courtesy of NBC.

★

Scorpion still courtesy of CBS.

The Haunted Hathaways still courtesy of Nickelodeon.

The Big Bang Theory still courtesy of CBS.

Spooksville still courtesy of Hub Network.

The Roloffs photo courtesy of The Learning Channel.

Power Rangers Super Mega Force photo courtesy of Nickelodeon.

About a Boy still courtesy of NBC.

The Thundermans photo courtesy of Nickelodeon.

Chuck photo courtesy of NBC.

Continuum still courtesy of Syfy channel.

The Tomorrow People still courtesy of the CW.

Heroes still courtesy of NBC.

The Flash still courtesy of the CW.

Journey photo courtesy of Hallmark Hall of Fame.

"One Foot" still courtesy of Fueled by Ramen.

"So Far Away" still courtesy of Avenged Sevenfold.

"Converse Girl" still courtesy of The Buttons Music.

"You're Only Human (Second Wind)" still courtesy of Columbia.

Traveler album cover photo and lyrics from "Joe Kelly's Shoes," courtesy of Sugar Hill Records.

Chapter 6

Dave Maddocks quote from Tanika White, "'Chuck' Taylors for the Cool and the Too-Cool-to-be-Cool," *Baltimore Sun*, August 6, 2004.

Jim Calhoun quote and San Francisco store photos from 2015 and 2013 Converse press releases.

★

Hal Peterson is one of the many chucks-wearers whom this book is about. He also is the web-master for **The ChucksConnection**, the world's largest website dedicated to the Chuck Taylor shoe. **The ChucksConnection** was started as a fun site, a way of exchanging information and photos about chucks between Peterson and other Internet acquaintances. Peterson was surprised to find that there were so many other people in the world who shared the same interest and passion for Chuck Taylors, and since it first went public in 1998, the site has continued to grow in content and sales.

Dr. Peterson completed undergraduate work at San Jose State University followed by graduate studies at Stanford University that was funded by a Ford Foundation grant. He taught classes in computers and music for thirty-five years in the south San Francisco Bay Area, designing innovative curriculum in the arts using technology. Since retiring from teaching, his focus is on creative projects as a writer and musician.

The ChucksConnection is a division of Hal Peterson Media Services, a business that operates educational and commercial websites, produces music arrangements and publications, and publishes the *Hunter & Holmes Mystery Series*, which is about two chucks-wearing teenaged detectives living in the Silicon Valley.

Made-in-USA navy-blue high-top chucks.

Wheel of high-top chucks in seasonal colors.